DESIGN BY IKEA

DESIGN BY IKEA

A CULTURAL HISTORY

SARA KRISTOFFERSSON

Translated by William Jewson

B L O O M S B U R Y

LONDON • NEW DELHI • NEW YORK • SYDNEY

Bloomsbury Academic

An imprint of Bloomsbury Publishing Plc

50 Bedford Square	1385 Broadway
London	New York
WC1B 3DP	NY 10018
UK	USA

www.bloomsbury.com

Bloomsbury is a registered trade mark of Bloomsbury Publishing Plc

First published 2014

British Library Cataloguing-in-Publication Data
A catalogue record for this book is available from the British Library.

ISBN: HB: 978-0-8578-5813-9
PB: 978-0-8578-5814-6
ePDF: 978-1-4725-8737-4
ePub: 978-0-8578-5815-3

Library of Congress Cataloging-in-Publication Data
A catalogue record for this book is available from the Library of Congress.

Typeset by RefineCatch, Bungay, Suffolk
Printed and bound in India

CONTENTS

ILLUSTRATIONS

Plates

Figures

ACKNOWLEDGMENTS

This book was written as part of a research project entitled *Svensk design? Om Ikeas estetik på 1980-och 90-talet. Export av 'svensk design' och nationella myter* [Swedish design? Ikea's aesthetics in the 1980s and 1990s. The exportation of 'Swedish Design' and national myths]. The project is funded by the Swedish Foundation for Humanities and Social Sciences. I am also indebted to the following for financial assistance: Torsten Söderbergs Stiftelse, Estrid Ericson Stiftelse, Åke Wibergs Stiftelse and Stiftelsen San Michele. I should also like to thank Kim Salomon for scrutinizing the manuscript and for his invaluable comments.

Please note that Inter IKEA Systems B.V. is the exclusive proprietor of all rights in and to the IKEA Retail Systems, which includes the IKEA trademarks, throughout the world. The Company name, the term "IKEA", and all related names, logos, product and service names, designs and slogans are trademarks of Inter IKEA Systems B.V. Images and trademarks from IKEA Retail Systems are used in this publication by kind permission of Inter IKEA Systems B.V.

1

CONFIGURING IKEA

'Why is the Swedish team sponsored by IKEA?' a Spanish gentleman wondered while attending the Euro 2012 football championship in the summer of 2012.[1] The Swedish team's blue and yellow kit clearly triggered associations with IKEA, rather than with the Swedish flag. One is prompted to ask whether IKEA has actually outgrown Sweden in the public consciousness.

IKEA does not merely sell design. It sells Sweden and, indeed, Scandinavia too. Few international brands have such an explicitly national profile. IKEA has made 'Swedishness' a virtue in itself, as well as an essential aspect of its strategy for the brand. The blue and yellow logotype alludes to the Swedish flag, while the products have names that associate them with Sweden or Scandinavia; and Swedish food is served in IKEA's restaurants under the device 'A Taste of Sweden.' It is not just a matter of aesthetic and concrete references, for IKEA also makes use of more abstract notions about Swedish society and Swedish design.

There are, for example, constant references to an image of Sweden as suffused with social and economic equality and an equally traditional notion as to what really characterizes Swedish design. Has IKEA adopted Swedish values and has it developed a corporate ideology that includes social and political consciousness, or is this a matter of cynically exploiting Swedish culture and fundamental Swedish values? One readily forms the impression that IKEA is driven by a social and democratic pathos, though the business strategy is, of course, primarily dictated by crass financial self-interest.

Neither aspect excludes the other. The goal of increased sales does not exclude a sense of social responsibility. Making use of a national identity as a resource and a sales pitch is neither particularly dramatic nor uncommon. But one can reflect upon the consequences. Underlying the narratives there are commercial impulses, but it would be an oversimplification to dismiss these as innocuous. The financial interest does not drastically reduce the impact of the message and, accordingly, the setting and the rhetoric cannot be ignored. On the contrary, the use of such narratives in IKEA's marketing strategy helps to establish our view of the past and our understanding of the present. Those responsible for the narrative do not need to have political, cultural or ideological intentions for their narratives to have an impact beyond the purely commercial. What we believe, know and imagine has largely been shaped by various narratives. We are not just influenced by the daily assault of news through the media but, possibly to a greater extent, by advertising, films and computer games. For example, a fictional TV series like 'The West Wing' has a greater impact on how people view American politics than what actually takes place in the political sphere. Actual power and influence over an individual's ideas and opinions do not always have to be regarded as intentional or as the result of a conscious strategy.

Popular culture is a genre of its own but it also contributes to our view of society in general. In the years since the millennium, 'soft power' has become an increasingly central term for explaining political influence. Soft power distinguishes itself from traditional concepts like military and economic power. The term was minted by Joseph Nye and is concerned with an ability to generate sympathy and to appeal to people by means of attractive narratives, consumption and culture. Nye maintains that, in our own time, it is a question of which narrative wins and so occasional symbolic gestures and actions mean more that traditional political activities.[2]

This book is concerned with a global brand that impacts on how the world regards Sweden and Swedish design but that is also important to how Swedes view themselves. Determining a company's nationality is difficult in our globalized existence. In the case of IKEA, it is clear that the concept and the brand are owned by Inter IKEA Systems B.V. which is registered in the Netherlands, while most of the products are manufactured far beyond Sweden's borders, frequently in low-wage countries. That IKEA functions as Sweden's face in the world as well as a symbol of Sweden is not just a role that the company has assumed voluntarily. In Sweden IKEA is proudly regarded as a sort of national symbol, and even though there is little in IKEA's corporate structure that has anything to do with Sweden, the company still receives a helping hand from the Swedish authorities.

For decades IKEA has taken advantage of established notions about Sweden as a democratic and egalitarian welfare state. The company's narrative has acquired a certain standing and a degree of official legitimacy. Indeed, on occasions IKEA has been chosen to represent Sweden and to shape notions about Swedish society and Swedish design. And so it is important to ask ourselves which narrative is being promoted, as well as reflecting on the fact that a commercial brand can play such an important role in promoting the image of a country's culture, ideology and politics. Fundamentally it is a matter of how the conception of Sweden and Swedish design are renegotiated and shaped by a corporate culture.

Yet another aspect that prompts this book is the fact that IKEA has largely 'written its own history' without encountering any serious friction. The historical narratives are then credulously repeated by the media and in surveys of design history. By partially financing exhibitions and books about the company, IKEA has been able to retain an influence on its own historical narrative which is then adopted and reproduced by other people in other contexts.[3]

A furniture company's history and legitimacy

The subject of this book is IKEA. But IKEA is a gigantic organization. Not just in itself but in the material pertaining to it. The company was registered as a business in 1943 by a seventeen-year-old Ingvar Kamprad. In the space of few decades it developed into one of the world's leading furniture manufacturers. Initially Kamprad sold all sorts of wares including matches and pens, but he soon decided to concentrate on home furnishings. IKEA is an acronym made up of the founder's initials together with the initial letters of the names of Elmtaryd and Agunnaryd, the farm and the village where he grew up.

IKEA started to sell so-called 'knock-down furniture' by mail-order back in 1956. This was furniture that was delivered in a package and that customers assembled themselves from parts. Two years later the doors opened at the first IKEA shop located in the small southern Swedish town of Älmhult. In 1965 a flagship store was opened at Kungens Kurva in the south of Stockholm. The first store outside Scandinavia opened in Switzerland in 1973 and, in the same decade, a succession of stores was established in different parts of Europe. The international expansion continued throughout the 1980s at the same time that a complicated corporate structure developed. Inter IKEA Systems B.V. owns the concept and the brand. Each new store is meticulously planned by Inter IKEA which is also responsible for training management and staff, as well as ensuring that the store adheres to the concept which requires following all sorts of regulations and guidelines for running an IKEA store. In 2013 there were 298 stores in more than thirty-eight countries, and the annual turnover, according to company accounts, amounted to €27.7 billion.[4]

IKEA's exceptional success and the size of the company have attracted the attention of scholars, particularly in the field of business studies which have focused on the internal organization of the company and Kamprad's unusual management style.[5] One central interest is in determining what factors have led to this success which is generally explained in terms of well-developed logistics and a highly distinctive business model. But IKEA's success is also attributed to the strong corporate culture.

One early study (1990) analyzed the values and visions that have permeated the organization. Researchers maintained that Kamprad's opinions and approach provided guidelines for how the staff should act and that the leader came to be regarded as a sort of cohesive cement. Since the corporate culture was seen as being linked up with the founder's innovative and unconventional style of leadership the question also arose as to how IKEA would be able to continue to grow and flourish without Kamprad's leadership.[6]

There can be no doubt that both the corporate culture at IKEA and Ingvar Kamprad himself have played an important part in the company's success, but there is much to suggest that the narrative of organization and the brand are of greater significance.[7] In an influential and penetrating field study entitled *Identity Across Borders: A Study in the 'IKEA-World'* (1994), Miriam Salzer studied IKEA as a culture in which norms and ideas were implanted with the help of the staff's own narratives that exist at different levels and in different contexts within the company. Symbols, culture and identity are seen as parts of a process that is constantly developing within the organization.[8]

Narratives have not just been important internally, but have also been central elements of external communication. They have acted, inside and outside the company, as a form of linguistic artifacts that give expression to the brand and testify as to what IKEA is and wants to be. Of great significance is the success story that explains how and why the company was started. Taken together, the stories form a narrative which is neither static nor permanent. Rather, there is a living narrative that is constantly tended and redrafted. New chapters are written, not only by IKEA itself but also by customers and media, and this reproduces the narrative, keeping the mythology and the story of the brand alive. The narrative has long been used in one way or another to establish unity or identity, which can be likened to what Benedict Anderson classes as 'an imagined community.' This community builds on a sense of connectedness with people who one neither knows nor will ever get to know. The basis for the sense of being connected lies, precisely, in the notion of forming part of a community.[9]

The company is no exception here, but the narratives—whether true or false—are used to attract customers, to create a sense of community and identity, and to motivate the staff. But while the concept of 'storytelling' is general in application, the notion of 'corporate storytelling' more specifically refers to narration within organizations and businesses in both internal and external contexts.[10] In brief, it is a matter of using narratives to establish norms and values, goals and visions among the staff as well as providing a strategic tool for communicating with customers.

The success of the chain of stores is often explained in terms of well-developed logistics, a potent corporate culture, and Kamprad's curious style of leadership. Flat packs and low prices are other common explanations. But as we have already mentioned, the starting point for this particular book is in the narratives that have played a central role in IKEA's success story. That companies make use of narratives both internally and externally in building their brands is in no sense unique to IKEA. The fundamental question in this book is, rather, concerned with what it is that makes IKEA's narratives so effective.

My aim is not to identify the recipe for IKEA's success. Rather, it is to analyze and deconstruct IKEA's narratives in order to explain why these particular narratives have been so extraordinarily effective. Several questions need to be answered: Is there some form of guiding principle or recurring Ur-narrative? What is emphasized and what do the narratives refrain from mentioning? How have the narratives been shaped, used and handed on?

IKEA's use of Sweden and Swedish design is hardly the result of free fantasies but is firmly secured in established notions and in the real world. The mild, virgin countryside of Sweden that is portrayed in emotive photographs of the company in catalogs and on IKEA's website certainly exist. There are mooses there too. And mooses frequently stop and stare in the middle of a road. Blond, blue-eyed people do live in Sweden and social issues play an important role in political debate.

This book does not seek to determine whether IKEA's narratives are an accurate reflection of reality or not. My ambition is, rather, to identify the content of the narratives. The analysis also includes relating them to contrasting narratives as well as direct criticism. The aim is not, fundamentally, concerned with the truth of the stories, nor of refuting or destroying the company's narratives but, rather, in explaining why they appear as they do and how they have been shaped, as well as the reasons for their success.

The limits of the chosen period run from the late 1970s, when IKEA was 'Swedicized,' to the 2000s with the focus on the 1980s and 1990s. Clearly, the profile has not always been Swedish. In the 1950s, for example, the brand name was actually spelt with an accent in a French idiom: Ikéa. It was in connection with IKEA's international expansion that the Swedish identity was emphasized in order to create a more distinct and coherent profile. In parallel with its growth, IKEA began to formulate its history, origins and identity strategically. Courses were organized to teach employees about the firm's values and the importance of its heritage in rural Sweden. That IKEA was not just any capitalist corporation, but that it was inspired by a social mission was stressed, not least, in a creation story as to how and why the business had been started.[11]

Reality itself is always adapted and edited in every narrative or history. There may be much in a narrative that is true. But reality can also be renegotiated dramaturgically. Situations and facts are shaped to make a good story. Thus it is not the range of products, not the furniture and design items as such, that are the focus but the narratives of the range and the brand. The approach distinguishes itself from histories of design based on material considerations which are primarily concerned with artifacts, their methods of manufacture, materials and design.[12] Rather, it is the context, the discourse and rhetoric attaching to the company's products as well as Swedish design in general that is of interest. And so I have concentrated on the notions, histories and fictions pertaining to IKEA's design, rather than the artifacts themselves.

Discourse analysis is a wide-ranging concept. In the present book, narrative theory is central. IKEA does not just produce designs in the form of products but also 'fabricates' narratives which, in turn, draw substance from other narrative descriptions. In other words it is a question of a narrower spectrum of the company's activities, though a spectrum which is central to understanding the IKEA brand and the company's success. The point of departure and the interpretation demand a broader approach with detours into politics and history, for example. In order to analyze the issues treated in the book we need to move between different fields, using theoretical perspectives from a variety of disciplines. As Elizabeth Wilson has pointed out in connection with fashion history, it is difficult to understand the complexity of the subject and its links with, for example, politics, gender and economics if one studies it in isolation.[13] One can inspect the seams but the context is the decisive element.

Facts and fictions

National characteristics and markers have long been used by governments and corporations in positioning themselves. This is largely a matter of emphasizing attractive characteristics in order to profile oneself in relation to others. But we have to ask whether design really has national overtones. My argument takes the view that it is notions, histories and fictions about what characterizes Swedish design that directs the interpretation rather than any specific and innate properties.

The concept of 'Swedish Modern' is a good example. The term was minted in the 1930s to describe a gentler version of a modernist idiom: wood instead of metal tubing, organic forms rather than hard and angular designs. The style was synchronized with Sweden's political mainstream and the concept is regularly taken up as an example of the international success of Swedish designers. But as art historian Jeff Werner has indicated, the concept was most often used to describe furniture manufactured in the USA and designed by American designers. In other words, it was the narratives of the nation itself and of Swedish design, rather than the design itself, that made this style Swedish.[14]

That language is fundamental to our understanding of reality is an established hypothesis in postmodern discourse. True, people perceive the world in many different ways, but the point is that our perceptions of past and present are influenced by stories, images, metaphors and words that help to explain what would otherwise be an incalculably complex and fragmented world. The narratives scarcely reproduce reality like a blueprint but simplify and refine our perceptions. Also important in this context are: who is responsible for the narrative and what are their aims.

It is a well-established truth that companies do not just produce material artifacts or offer services, but that they also create brands that are by no means confined merely to a logotype and a product. Competition between manufacturers is no longer just a matter of price and quality but also of corporate narratives. Business has changed in step with a shift from focus on actual, material goods to immaterial aspects. Branding also includes feelings, ideas, images and stories.[15] There is no fixed meaning as such, no permanent content but constant change according to time and context.

As brands have developed into more than just a label, the importance of brands and branding has spiraled. In psychology identity has long been interpreted as a consistent and coherent ego but, in more recent times, has been defined as something that develops rather than something that is. Accordingly, there is simply no ego to manifest but it can, on the other hand, be constructed. Of course a brand identity can be understood in similar fashion. Companies commit major resources to building and preserving their identity. With the help of narratives about values and characteristics and conscious management of elements such as graphic design a 'personality,' a distinct and unique identity is created.

Branding is, quite simply, a matter of defining what one is in order to distinguish and position oneself in the market. It is a matter of values and meanings, in addition to the company's products or services, that are communicated by stories and images. How the brand is actually perceived is not, of course, the same as how the brand seeks to be understood. There can be a large discrepancy between how a company formulates its identity and how this identity is actually received. Thus the images and narratives that companies construct to describe themselves can differ from those actually generated in the recipient's consciousness.

During the 1990s there was increasing corporate interest in dramaturgical notions and so-called corporate storytelling became increasingly popular. The economic potential of a good story was emphasized and management consultants claimed that brands should be launched and organizations should be described using narratives. In the public domain they are used as marketing tools while internally they are a way of strengthening the corporate culture and promoting a sense of community among employees. American management and marketing books in particular, with titles such as *Shakespeare on Management* (1999) and *The Classic Touch: Lessons in Leadership from Homer to Hemingway* (1999) testify to inspiration from the literary world.[16] The pervading opinion shared by advocates of the policy is that narratives are more effective than information communicated in traditional ways. The key to success is, quite simply, considered to be a good story. Or as Rolf Jensen put it in his book *The Dream Society* (1999): 'whoever tells the best story, and whoever tells it the best, will win.'[17] The superiority of the genre has also been explained with the idea that conviction is the core to all forms of successful business activities, and that if one is to convince people one has to know how to tell a story.[18]

In practice it is a matter of reshaping and systematizing a company's history and strategy to provide a narrative. In order to arouse feelings and to distinguish oneself from competitors, products and traditions are woven into the story with the aim of captivating and engaging the public. Facts become meaningful and are easier to remember and to relate to when they are part of a narrative since the narrative is understood in a context. In our modern economies, in which the consumption of goods, lifestyles and dreams take up a lot of room, storytelling has, accordingly, become very much a matter of 'storyselling.'[19]

A corporate narrative is generally concerned with how and why the company was founded, what it stands for today and its visions for the future. Most people would agree that a narrative is a construction, but there are different opinions as to the role that the actual situation should play in this context. While some people consider that reality ought to be central to the narrative, others maintain that the main thing is that the narratives appear to be genuine and that they make an impression of authenticity.[20]

In *Storytelling. Bewitching the Modern Mind* (2010), Christian Salmon opines that storytelling, which is motivated instrumentally and commercially, has also left its mark on the political sphere. He shows how the phenomenon has developed in marketing in the USA and in French politics. According to Salmon, underlying this sort of success-oriented storytelling is a greater awareness and cynicism than we find in literature and in classical myths. Thus the narrative approach is consciously employed as an instrument for exercising power and influence.[21]

Marketing of nations, regions and cities has long existed, but an understanding of branding has become increasingly important. There is fierce competition in the global arena and it is not just in the corporate sector that organizations are seeking to shape their identity. Countries, too, invest large sums of money in creating or strengthening their national identities.[22]

Research into the use of such narratives has increased in parallel with the growth of interest in corporate storytelling. The starting point for such research lies in an understanding that history can be shaped, can be created, and can be used for a variety purposes, and that it is truly a product of its own time. As long ago as the nineteenth century Friedrich Nietzsche devoted himself to the study of what history can be used for.[23] Inspired by German philosophy and the classification of how we master and are mastered by history, Klas-Göran Karlsson has developed a typology of seven ways of using history: scientific, existential, moral, ideological, non-use, educationally political and commercial.[24] In this context it is primarily the commercial use of history that is interesting. This can be traced in films, in fiction, in magazines and in advertising and it reaches a large audience. Thus the commercial use of history clearly influences our view of the past and Karlsson poses the somewhat rhetorical question: 'What happens to history in popular culture?' Does the holocaust become Americanized on its way to Hollywood because it is furnished with American and commercial values that, at times, can be almost impossible to conceive: like a happy ending?[25]

Corporate storytelling does not have to be backward looking, though the past frequently plays a central role. Advocates of what has been called 'History Marketing' emphasize the importance of preserving and communicating a company's history in order to strengthen and intensify the corporate culture. History is seen as a vital resource in the company's marketing strategy. One reason that has been put forward is that the company's history is unique and thus cannot be copied by competitors.[26] There are even companies that specialize in relating a company's history by organizing a museum, mounting exhibitions, organizing jubilee celebrations or writing a book devoted to the company's history. The US consultants 'The History Factory' claim that they can help to 'tell an organization's story with techniques as time-tested as Homer, Shakespeare and the latest Hollywood blockbuster. Our StoryARC™ methodology results in a narrative of your organization that is not only informative, but genuinely entertaining.'[27]

The self-image in a landscape of manuals

IKEA's own answer to the question of the company's success is that it is due to a special business idea and a concept that is regarded as holy: 'If we stick to the concept we will never die.'[28] The explanations point one to Pandora's famous box though in some respects there are no secrets. Everyone who visits an IKEA store can study the concept at close quarters. As with other multinational chain stores, the same sales principles apply throughout the world. Thus the legendary concept can be partially defined as a business model which can be rented for a franchise fee.

On the company's intranet one can find the heading 'The IKEA Manual Landscape.' The heading hides a rigorous list of directives covering everything from how the logotype is to be used to what a complete IKEA store is to look like in order to function optimally. There are also manuals describing the brand identity, how this should be used and how it is to be marketed. The material is not classified as secret but the manuals of guidelines are intended for use within the corporation. The manuals cover such issues as how IKEA wants to be perceived, that is its self-image and its narrative which is, of course, not the same thing.

That a product has the same name and appearance all over the globe does not mean that it has the same significance everywhere, nor that it is understood in the same way globally. How it is interpreted and understood must be seen in a perspective that includes cultural, economic and social factors. IKEA is by no means the only global brand that has different connotations in different parts of the globe. In poor countries Coca-Cola signals exclusivity while in the West it is connected with everyday life. One readily realizes that meanings change. The goal is to reach out as extensively as possible.

The brand's ambition is, accordingly, to create coherent narratives and a well-defined identity which can also be understood globally. IKEA's concept is communicated from the center, that is from Inter IKEA Systems B.V., to the individual stores. The company's images, symbols, words and metaphors are identical everywhere, but are understood by consumers not only in relation to national contexts but of course also in relation to class and cultural capital. In many parts of the world an IKEA store is associated with low prices, though the products are not as cheap for Russians as they are for Swedes.[29] For Russians the products and brand have greater status than for Swedes. And while IKEA's famous meatballs function as a sort of everyday nationalism to Swedes, people of other nationalities regard them as something exotic.

Globalization also encourages regional interpretations. As Anthony Giddens has noted, when customs, meanings and symbols are exchanged globally they are torn from their original context and they then establish themselves in the countries where they land; which results in a local translation.[30] In Germany, for example, there are deeply rooted notions about Sweden and an intense admiration of Swedish ideals, which has led to highly clichéd portrayals of that nation. The German TV series 'Inga Lindström' was filmed in the Swedish archipelago. All the characters are blond, drive Volvos and live in red houses flying blue and yellow flags from white poles. The veritable orgy of clichés can be a little too much for a Swede, but for a mass audience in Germany the series works as the model of a romantic view of Sweden.[31]

It is only a short step from here to IKEA's German TV advertising which frequently alludes to Swedish traditions, Nordic views on equality and progressive Swedish welfare policies.[32] For Germans, IKEA's blue and yellow colors and its frequent references to the Swedish countryside and to welfare say something very different from what they communicate to a Chinese audience. Of course IKEA's marketing is not the same all over the world. True, there are uniform guidelines for advertisements and commercials with clear definitions of the brand identity. But advertising is created by agencies in different countries, which means that marketing strategies can vary and can have local overtones or a national profile.[33]

IKEA's advertising has often challenged accepted conventions.[34] One notable example is the American commercial showing Steve and his male partner who are hunting for a new dining table while also challenging the American understanding of the family. While conservatives were scandalized, the commercial won approval in liberal circles.[35] It is hardly likely that this film would have worked as well in Saudi Arabia or in Russia.

My study touches on how IKEA has been received in various different countries, though it is the brand's self-image and the guidelines for how this is to be expressed that is the main focus. Comparing IKEA's advertising in different countries could widen one's perspective, particularly with regard to national elements in marketing strategies. So too would a study of the global reception of IKEA. How and why our understanding varies between countries and groups is, without a doubt, an interesting question but it would be a gigantic research project that is beyond the scope of this study.

Research on IKEA, as we have noted, is dominated by economic and organizational aspects, often with a focus on the internal activities of the company.[36] But there are many other more important issues pertaining to IKEA and by no means all of them are concerned with economics. In spite of IKEA's global diffusion, research into cultural aspects is limited. One of several explanations may be that the company was formerly rather reserved; another is the language barrier, since earlier materials are mainly in Swedish. This does not mean that the matter is totally unresearched and there is research based on a more cultural orientation. Both the American and the French perceptions of IKEA have been penetrated.[37] Many studies have a specific focus. One such study looks at how IKEA is perceived in the UK, or rather, what UK consumers regard as good value in furniture.[38] Another study compares how customers in Stockholm and Dublin view shopping at IKEA.[39] And catalogs from different periods have also been studied.[40] There are books about IKEA on a more general level too. Some of them are highly informative with regard to design and products, while others are more discursive, lacking critical distance. A considerable number of books about IKEA are written from an economic perspective with the focus on management.[41] There are books commissioned by IKEA while other books question the company or seek to confront it. *Historien om IKEA* (1998) by Bertil Torekull (*Leading By Design: The IKEA Story*) was commissioned by Kamprad and is an initiated but fairly deferential portrayal.[42] Journalist Thomas Sjöberg has written a much less respectful book in which he maps Kamprad's Nazi contacts based on earlier revelations of Kamprad's Nazi sympathies.[43] Just as critical is the book *The Truth About IKEA* (2010) which is a sort of kiss-and-tell story in which a former employee, Johan Stenebo, takes his former boss to task.[44]

In the present book, information from IKEA intended for the staff plays an essential role. This information is gleaned from publications dealing with sales methods, branding strategies, and goals and visions, as well as documenting IKEA's culture, tradition and history. I have had access to this material partly in IKEA's own archive and partly in the Royal Library in Stockholm. Originally the material was only available on paper in Swedish. More recent material can be found in English on IKEA's intranet to which all the company's employees have access. I have made use of both categories of information.

Other material is, so to speak, external and available to the public, containing information that IKEA has published as part of its marketing strategy. Important in this context are catalogs devoted to particular collections or products and books published in connection with various jubilees. I have also had access to material in Hans Brindfors' personal archive. Brindfors was head of the agency that IKEA used in the initial phase of international expansion.

Where the material is only available in Swedish, references are translated into English. Where IKEA's own texts are available in English these are used throughout the book. Readers should note that IKEA's English texts are idiosyncratic with regard to language usage. This distinctive use of English can be seen as a conscious strategy on the part of the company to appear genuine and unaffected.

The library and archive of Sweden's Ministry for Foreign Affairs have also provided material for my analysis of the relation between IKEA and Sweden in the international arena. I have also conducted a number of interviews which have been important from two perspectives. They have provided information not otherwise available and this has proved helpful in generating insights and establishing perspectives. Basically, all of the people interviewed currently have or have had leading positions in IKEA with a focus on branding and corporate culture.

The book is arranged thematically within an overall chronology. In chapter two the focus is on IKEA's striking role as a storytelling organization. Of central interest is the store's basic narrative which can be seen as a sort of foundation or nucleus. Oral tradition within the company has been important but external marketing has also contributed to the mythology. One prominent element of the narrative is Sweden itself, and in chapter three I analyze which type of Swedishness is reflected in IKEA's rhetoric. I also show how the product range is exploited in order to promote the sense of Swedishness.

The fourth chapter considers the actual importance of the stores for the Swedish brand. IKEA excellently illustrates the fact that brands often play an important part in nation branding. The IKEA story and Swedish design are espoused though they differ from other representations. Chapter five of the book analyzes the company's own self-image, relating it to direct criticism. The concluding chapter takes as its starting point the fact that IKEA is part of our modern consumer culture while also presenting a summary of the book's conclusion.

Notes

1 Related by a member of the public at session with Sara Kristoffersson, 'Sweden designed by IKEA.' Paper presented at Culture Politics and Cultural Policies, VII International Conference on Cultural Policy Research, Barcelona, 2012.

2 Joseph Nye, *Soft Power: The Means to Success in World Politics* (New York: Perseus Books, 2004).

3 One example is the exhibition *Open me* shown at Kulturhuset in Stockholm 2001. The exhibition was produced in connection with IKEA launching its catalog and it reflected the year's theme: storage. Staffan Kihlström, 'IKEA, Rörstrand och IT-företag har ställt ut,' *Dagens Nyheter*, January 1, 2007. In 2009 IKEA financed an exhibition at the Liljevalchs municipal art gallery in Stockholm. This is discussed in chapter 6.

4 Company information at http://www.IKEA.com/ms/sv_SE/about-the-IKEA-group/company-information/index.html (accessed October 29, 2013).

5 IKEA is quoted as a successful example in several business-economics studies. Among the earlier ones are Michael E. Porter, 'What is Strategy?,' *Harvard Business Review*, Nov–Dec, 1996; Richard Normann and Rafael Ramirez, 'Designing Interactive Strategy: From Value Chain to Value Constellation,' *Harvard Business Review*, July, 1993, pp. 107–117; Sumantra Ghoshal and Christopher A. Bartlett, *The Individualized Corporation. A Fundamentally New Approach to Management. Great Companies are Defined by Purpose, Process, and People* (New York: HarperBusiness, 1997).

6 Christopher A. Bartlett and Ashish Nanda, *Ingvar Kamprad and IKEA* (Harvard Business School Case 390–132, 1990).

7 This is also noted by Lars Strannegård, 'Med uppdrag att berätta,' in Anders Dahlvig, *Med uppdrag att växa. Om ansvarsfullt företagande* (Lund: Studentlitteratur, 2011), p. 18.

8 The business study was inspired by ethnology/anthropology. Salzer uses participatory observation at stores in Sweden, France and Canada to analyze how members of a company constructed an organizational identity in an international context. Miriam Salzer, *Identity Across Borders: A Study in the 'IKEA-World,'* Diss. (Linköping: 1994), pp. 7–14, 16. See also Miriam Salzer-Mörling, *Företag som kulturella uttryck* (Bjärred: Academia adacta, 1998).

9 Benedict Anderson was primarily interested in notions about a joint nation and he described the national aspect as being imaginary ideas about collective belonging. Benedict Anderson, *Imagined Communities. Reflections on the Origin and Spread of Nationalism* (Verso, London, 1983).

10 Literature in this field also uses the term 'business narrative,' though less frequently than 'corporate storytelling.' David M. Boje, Yiannis Gabriel and Barbara Czarniawska are leading exponents of storytelling research in management and organization research. See David M. Boje, 'Stories of the Storytelling Organization: A Postmodern Analysis of Disney as "Tamara-Land"', *Academy of Management Journal*, Vol. 38, No. 4 (1995); Yiannis Gabriel, *Storytelling in Organizations: Facts, Fictions, and Fantasies* (Oxford: Oxford University Press, 2000); Barbara Czarniawska, *Narrating the Organization: Dramas on Institutional Identity* (Chicago: University of

Chicago Press 1997); Hilary McLellan, 'Corporate Storytelling Perspectives,' *Journal for Quality & Participation*, Vol. 29, No. 1 (2006).

11 The narrative was written by Leon Nordin and has been published in several editions, with minor alterations since 1984, and in a variety of languages. This book quotes from the English edition of 2008; *The Future is Filled With Opportunities. The Story Behind the Evolution of the IKEA Concept*, Inter IKEA Systems B.V. (2008) [1984] (IHA).

12 A succession of questions about the character of the subject have been discussed in recent decades: Is design history an academic discipline in its own right? How extensive is the field? Does it have its own methodology? In earlier times the subject was dominated by questions of style and taste but it is now regarded as interdisciplinary. For example, rather than dealing with the heroic contributions of particular designers, the subject often embraces everything in our everyday environment and material culture. The discipline developed in the 1970s and 1980s, not least through the foundation of *The Design History Society* in 1977. For a survey and discussion of the development of the subject, including theories and methods, see Kjetil Fallan, *Design History. Understanding Theory and Method* (Oxford: Berg, 2010). For essential discussion of the subject in the 1980s and 1990s, see Grace Lees-Maffei and Rebecka Houze (eds), *The Design History Reader* (Oxford: Berg, 2010); Hazel Clark and David Brody (eds), *Design Studies. A Reader* (Oxford: Berg, 2009).

13 For a long period, fashion research was decidedly materialistic with the focus on individual fashion items and costume history. But fashion covers more than just items of clothing and there are far more people active in the field than merely fashion designers, including stylists, journalists, stores and public relations (PR) agencies, as well as consumers. See the introduction to Elisabeth Wilson, *Adorned in Dreams. Fashion and Modernity* (London: Virago, 1985). See also Yuniya Kawamura: *Fashion-ology. An Introduction to Fashion Studies* (Oxford: Berg, 2005).

14 Jeff Werner, *Medelvägens estetik. Sverigebilder i USA Del 1* (Hedemora/Möklinga: Gidlunds förlag, 2008), p. 289; Helena Kåberg, 'Swedish Modern. Selling Modern Sweden,' *Art Bulletin of Nationalmuseum*, 18 (2011), pp. 150–7.

15 There is extensive research on brands. A pioneering study of the historical roots of the logotype that emphasizes the fact that brands consist of more ingredients than the logo itself is Per Mollerup, *Marks of Excellence. The Function and Variety of Trademarks* (London: Phaidon, 1997). For a survey with a greater emphasis on sociological and cultural aspects see Jonathan E. Schroeder and Miriam Slazer-Mörling (eds), *Brand Culture* (London: Routledge, 2006).

16 Paul Corrigan, *Shakespeare on Management. Leadership Lessons for Today's Managers* (London: Kogan Page Business Books, 1999); John K. Clemens and Douglas F. Mayer, *The Classic Touch: Lessons in Leadership from Homer to Hemingway* (New York: McGraw-Hill, 1999).

17 Rolf Jensen: *The Dream Society. How the Coming Shift from Information to Imagination will Transform your Business* (New York: McGraw-Hill), 1999, p. 90.

18 Bronwyn Fryer, 'Storytelling That Moves People,' *Harvard Business Review*, June (2003). Robert McKee is a leading scriptwriter who has also been commissioned by companies to talk about storytelling. In the film *Adaptation*, in which Nicolas Cage plays a desperate scriptwriter he goes to a seminar led by McKee looking for help. *Adaptation*, Director Spike Jonze (2002).

19 Miriam Salzer-Mörling, 'Storytelling och varumärken' in Lars Christensen and Peter Kempinsky (eds), *Att mobilisera för regional tillväxt* (Lund: Studentlitteratur, 2004), p. 119.

20 Lena Mossberg and Erik Nissen Johansen, *Storytelling* (Lund: Studentlitteratur, 2006), pp. 159–65.

21 Christian Salmon, *Storytelling. Bewitching the Modern Mind* (London: Verso Books, 2010) [2007].

22 Wally Olins is one of the earliest advocates of branding and has pointed to the fact that nations and companies are increasingly reminiscent of each other. Wally Olins: *Trading Identities: Why Countries and Companies are Taking on Each Others' Roles* (London: Foreign Policy Centre, 1999).

23 As early as the end of the nineteenth century Friedrich Nietzsche divided history's uses into three headings: Monumental, in which history is used as a teacher, Antiquarian, in which history is used for preserving values and artifacts, and/or Critical, which embraces the need to put the past on trial. Friedrich Nietzsche, *The Use and Abuse of History* (New York: Cosimo, 2005) [1874].

24 Klas-Göran Karlsson and Ulf Zander (eds), *Historien är nu: En introduktion till historiedidaktiken* (Lund: Studentlitteratur, 2004), pp. 55–66. This is a further development of the topology Karlsson introduced in Klas-Göran Karlsson, *Historia som vapen: Historiebruk och Sovjetunionens upplösning 1985–1999* (Stockholm: Natur & Kultur, 1999).

25 Karlsson and Zander 2004, p. 68.

26 Wolfgang Hartwig and Alexander Schug, *History Sells!: Angewandte Geschichte ALS Wissenschaft Und Markt* (Stuttgart: Franz Steiner Verlag, 2009).

27 http://www.historyfactory.com/how-we-do-it/storytelling/ (accessed August 9, 2003).

28 Kamprad quoted in Bertil Torekull, *Historien om IKEA* (Stockholm: Wahlström & Widstrand, 2008) [1998], p. 153. There is an English edition of the book entitled *Leading by Design* (New York: Harper Collins, 1999). Since the English edition is somewhat abbreviated, I have chosen to use the original Swedish version.

29 Irina Sandomirskaja, 'IKEA's pererstrojka,' *Moderna Tider*, November (2000), pp. 54–7. See also Lennart Dahlgren, *IKEA älskar Ryssland. En berättelse om ledarskap, passion och envishet* (Stockholm: Natur & Kultur, 2009). Dahlgren was formerly on the staff of IKEA and was involved in establishing the company in Russia.

30 Anthony Giddens, *Modernity and Self-Identity: Self and Society in the Late Modern Age* (Cambridge: Polity Press, 1991).

31 Berthold Franke, 'Tyskarna har hittat sin Bullerbü,' *Svenska Dagbladet*, December 9, 2007.

32 Jennie Mazur, *Die 'schwedische' Lösung: Eine kultursemiotisch orientierte Untersuchung der audiovisuellen Werbespots von IKEA in Deutschland*, Diss. (Uppsala: Department of Modern Languages, Uppsala University, 2012).

33 Interview with Lismari Markgren, Inter IKEA Systems, Waterloo, January 4, 2011.

34 That IKEA's marketing is usually perceived as relatively provocative is generally noted in discussion of the company's advertising. See, for example, Elen Lewis, *Great IKEA! A Brand for All the People* (London: Marshall Cavendish, 2008), pp. 118–32.

35 Stellan Björk, *IKEA. Entreprenören. Affärsidén. Kulturen* (Stockholm: Svenska Förlaget, 1998), p. 266.

36 For example, the transmission of knowledge between members of the IKEA staff in conjunction with establishing the company in different countries has been studied, with a particular focus on Russia, China and Japan. Anna Jonsson, *Knowledge Sharing Across Borders—A Study in the IKEA World*, Diss. (Lund: Lund Business Press, 2007).

37 On IKEA in the USA see Jeff Werner, *Medelvägens estetik. Sverigebilder i USA Del 2*, Hedemora: Gidlunds, 2008), pp. 249–69. On IKEA in France see Tod Hartman, 'On the IKEAization of France,' Public Culture, Vol. 19, No. 3 (Duke University Press, 2007), pp. 483–98; Anders Björkvall, 'Practical Function and Meaning. A Case study of IKEA Tables' in Carey Jewitt (ed.), *The Routledge Handbook of Multimodal Analysis* (London: Routledge, 2009), pp. 242–52. The latter deals with how IKEA's tables have been used in Australian homes.

38 The study claims that the shopping experience is of great importance to how British consumers perceive IKEA. Frida Andersson, *Performing Co-Production. On the Logic and Practice of Shopping at IKEA*, Diss. (Uppsala: Department of Social and Economic Geography, 2009).

39 Pauline Garvey: 'Consuming IKEA. Inspiration as Material Form' in Alison J. Clarke (ed.), *Design Anthropology* (Wien, New York: Springer Verlag, 2010), pp. 142–53.

40 Hanna Lindberg, *Vastakohtien IKEA. IKEAn arvot ja mentaliteetti muuttuvassa ajassa ja ympäristössä*, Diss. (Jyväskylä: Jyväskylän yliopisto, 2006).

41 Eva Atle Bjarnestam, *IKEA. Design och identitet* (Malmö: Arena, 2009); Björk 1998; Dahlgren 2009; Lewis 2008. The latter book is concerned with design history but the author has not had access to internal documents, nor has interviewed members of the staff.

42 Torekull 2008.

43 Thomas Sjöberg, *Ingvar Kamprad och hans IKEA. En svensk saga* (Stockholm: Gedin, 1998).

44 Johan Stenebo, *Sanningen om IKEA* (Västerås: ICA Bokförlag, 2009).

2
ONCE UPON A TIME

'A long time ago a boy was born in a poor country called Småland (pronounced small-land).'[1] The IKEA creation story is like many other fables, and it permeates the corporate culture. Both within IKEA and in the world in general there are numerous parallel stories; in particular stories about sales strategies and products and, not least, about the founder's frugal lifestyle. IKEA is internationally recognized as a pioneer in corporate storytelling and this circumstance forms the starting point for the chapter.

There are two foundational narratives of IKEA: *The Testament of a Furniture Dealer* (1976) and *The Future is Filled with Possibilities* (1984).[2] These deal with how the company started and what it stands for (Figure 2.1). The anecdotes, myths and stories that circulate both within and without the company are generally based on and complement these two tales which thus form a sort of Ur-text.

IKEA's leading position in corporate storytelling raises a number of questions. What are the messages? How are they communicated? What types of narrative do they form? What significance have they had on the corporate culture? The company points to three important aspects of the operations: the business idea, the corporate culture, and the stores themselves together with the catalogs.[3]

That narratives play an important part becomes evident from the IKEA Culture Center in Älmhult (Figure 2.2). The center trains and imbues employees from all over the world in the company's culture and brand.[4] Just outside the entrance there is part of a stone wall. This is IKEA's symbol for hard work, thrift and perseverance; and another stone wall now surrounds the recently opened store in Älmhult.[5] The handle on the main door of the center is shaped like an enlarged version of the company's well-known hex or Allen key: 'The magic key. An important tool for democracy. The key that assembles IKEA furniture.'[6]

Inside the building there are lecture theaters, a complete collection of catalogs, maps showing all of the stores and interiors from various epochs. An interactive display, intended only for IKEA's employees, presents selected aspects of the operation with didactic explanations as to how and why things are done as they are. At the coffee machines, foreign guests can learn about the Swedish concept of 'FIKA [fee-KA] The Swedish coffee break is more than a coffee break. It is a ritual. . . .'[7]

Besides learning about everyday life in Sweden, visitors get to experience the culture of Småland by, for example, building a dry-stone wall, fishing for crayfish or visiting a local farm under the device: 'Experience Småland.' The point of these activities is that the participants, in very tangible fashion, should gain a more profound understanding of how the supposed Småland mentality and traditions have influenced the corporate culture.[8]

The future is filled with opportunities.

Or the philosophical story about IKEA.

For internal training – a part of The IKEA Way.

Figure 2.1 Cover, *The future is filled with opportunities*, 1984. The story was written by Leon Nordin at the Swedish advertising agency Brindfors and still functions as the company's history book. (Used with the permission of Inter IKEA Systems B.V. © Inter IKEA Systems B.V.)

Figure 2.2 IKEA Tillsammans, IKEA Cultural Center, Älmhult. (Used with the permission of Inter IKEA Systems B.V. © Inter IKEA Systems B.V.)

Above all, visitors are able to acquaint themselves with *The Testament of a Furniture Dealer*, which is the corporate culture's most important artifact.

Kamprad wrote his testament at a time when IKEA was planning for its international expansion and it can be regarded as an ideological and spiritual rampart which is constantly invoked in all sorts of situations. Within the company, the testament is regarded and referred to as a 'sacred record' and it begins with an overall vision which is constantly repeated: 'To create a better everyday life for the many people.'[9] The text comprises nine theses which summarize Kamprad's values and visions and, not least, the spirit that is to permeate the organization:

1. The product range—our identity.
2. The IKEA spirit. A strong and living reality.
3. Profit gives us resources.
4. Reaching good results with small means.
5. Simplicity is a virtue.
6. Doing it a different way.
7. Concentration—important to our success.

8.   Taking responsibility—a privilege.

9.   Most things still remain to be done. A glorious future!

The most central message of Kamprad's testament is that the company and the staff have a mission. Kamprad emphasizes the importance of profit for the survival and development of the company but does not use purely financial incentives for leading and inspiring the staff. He constantly reiterates the idea that the enthusiasm of the staff should be motivated by the overall ambition of bringing improvements to the daily lives of the average person: 'The aim of our effort to build up financial resources is to reach a good result in the long term.'[10]

In retrospect we can see that, since Kamprad wrote his testament, the company has developed into a large-scale and highly efficient international organization with all the institutionalization and complexity that is an unavoidable result. But the testament also shows that Kamprad seems to dream of, and to nurture the idea of his staff being loyal and idealistic just as though IKEA were a small company. If this is to be achieved, then there needs to be a lot of team spirit and commitment. Camaraderie and familiarity, solidarity and equality are key concepts: 'the readiness to give each other a helping hand with everything; the art of managing on small means, of making the best of what we had; cost-consciousness to the point of being stingy; humbleness, undying enthusiasm and the wonderful sense of community through thick and thin.'[11]

According to Kamprad's testament, everyone is regarded as part of the organization: 'Be thankful to those who are the pillars of our society! Those simple quiet, taken-for-granted people who always are willing to lend a helping hand.'[12] But it is equally important that every employee should be cost-conscious, which is to say, thrifty: 'That is our secret. That is the foundation of our success.'[13] The aim is to squeeze prices so that even people with very limited means can afford to shop at IKEA: 'Wasting resources is a mortal sin at IKEA.'[14] This entails not just being thrifty with economic resources but in behaving in a modest and unpretentious manner: 'Simplicity in our behavior gives us strength . . . We do not need fancy cars, posh titles, tailor-made uniforms or other status symbols. We rely on our own strength and our own will!'[15]

Kamprad writes of a 'we' and an 'us' and he emphasizes how different IKEA is. In his view, IKEA is not like other companies and the staff are expected to contribute new ideas and to be slightly daring: 'We dare to do things differently! Not just in large matters, but in solving small everyday problems too . . . Our protest against convention is not protest for its own sake: it is a deliberate expression of our constant search for development and improvement.'[16] Daring to go against the current requires initiative and a degree of courage. A fear of making a mistake should not be a hindrance: 'Only while sleeping one makes no mistakes . . . The fear of making mistakes is the root of bureaucracy and the enemy of development.'[17]

The ninth and last thesis of Kamprad's testament is concerned with self-discipline and unity and is a celebration of a sort of boundless optimism. The author grandiloquently exclaims: 'Let us continue to be a group of positive fanatics who stubbornly and persistently refuse to accept the impossible, the negative. What we want to do, we can do and will do together. A glorious future!'[18]

The Testament of a Furniture Dealer clearly shows that Kamprad developed a uniquely personal business ideology at an early stage and that his style of leadership was highly distinctive. With its evangelical fervor, the text is evocative of Biblical commandments or a catechism. There are constant exclamation marks, the tone is salvific and the rhetoric is reminiscent of a sermon or a political speech. Associations with religious or martial phenomena are not unusual in books about IKEA in which authors draw parallels with both Old and New Testaments as well as with Lutheran morality. At an earlier stage an employee likened IKEA to the sacred trinity. 'Father, Sons, and the Holy Anders [a former CEO].'[19]

The concept is described as 'holy,' staff training as 'Bible school,' employees are equated with 'commandos' and 'commercial cowboys' and Kamprad is likened to the Pope: '[IKEA] functions like the Vatican functions for the Catholic Church. It ensures that the correct faith is practised in the purchasing temples of the market.'[20]

In the mid-1980s the testament was refined into a short version entitled *IKEA in a Nutshell* (1984).[21] The text was equipped with *A Little IKEA Dictionary* (1984) in which particularly important words and concepts were explained at greater length in order to avoid misunderstandings: 'Humbleness, Willpower, Simplicity, The many people, Making do, Experience, Doing it a different way, Never say never, Fear of making mistakes, Status.'[22] The bottom line is known as 'The IKEA Way: the sum total of all of our values; the amalgamation of everything we believe in.'[23]

The concept of 'The IKEA Way' besides summarizing the IKEA philosophy, is also the title of the company's staff training course which was held, for the first time, in 1986.[24] The course was based on Kamprad's testament and, in due course, the nine theses were expanded with a history of how IKEA became IKEA under the heading: *The Future is Filled with Possibilities. Or the Philosophical Story about IKEA* (1984).[25]

The story of IKEA

The Future is Filled with Possibilities was written by Leon Nordin at the Swedish advertising agency Brindfors. Collaboration with Brindfors began in 1979 and *The Future is Filled with Possibilities* still functions as the company's history book, answering questions such as when, where, how and why IKEA was started. This narrative appears in other contexts too and in versions of varying lengths.[26] But a summary using Nordin's words and his approach goes something like this:

> The boy who was born in the poor Swedish province of Småland was called Ingvar Kamprad. When he was still only a child he determined to earn his own living. The boy had an eye for business and saw neither problems nor hindrances, only solutions and possibilities. Soon he could be seen out on his bike selling matches, Christmas decorations, packets of seeds, pens and watches.
>
> The pens proved to be an unsuspected success. His business grew so much that he needed a name for it and he called it IKEA: an acronym of his first name, his family name and the initials of the family farm's name together with the name of his village. A few years later he expanded the business into a mail-order company. Parcels were

picked up by the milk lorry and deposited at the railway station. In due course the milk round was altered and it was no longer possible to send his parcels with it.

Fortunately there was an old joinery factory for sale in the nearest little town. The young man bought the factory, making his first major investment in the company that now began to take shape. In the district there were several furniture factories run by thrifty and hardworking people from Småland and their products soon began to fill the pages of Kamprad's mail-order catalog.

That the furniture manufacturers were thrifty suited Kamprad perfectly, for low prices were important to his business idea from an early stage. Unfortunately, the furniture was clumsy and difficult to freight. Kamprad had once again run into a problem but, as with all such problems, he found a solution: 'It must, of course, be possible to assemble the furniture.'[27] During the 1950s IKEA started to sell furniture for customer-assembly that came in flat packages. The store in Älmhult became a popular destination for people from all over Sweden. Here one could inspect all the products that were featured in the catalog and could take them home on the car's roof rack.

But there was one cloud on the horizon. Traditional furniture dealers felt threatened by IKEA's low prices and tried to repel the young furniture dealer, for example by boycotting him at furniture fairs. But, as in the past, Kamprad found an alternative. He started his own design department and found suppliers in Eastern Europe. IKEA chose its own path and in the same spirit opened a store in Stockholm in 1965.

Instead of opening a shop on an exclusive street, IKEA built a giant store right by the motorway on the outskirts of Stockholm. Added to which the building was round. The store became a success, but problems arose on the very first day of trading. There were so many customers that there were serious delays while staff fetched items from the warehouse: 'What to do?'[28] The warehouse was opened to customers who collected products themselves. The notion of self-service was born. Once again IKEA had faced a problem and turned it into a friend.

Soon the idea arose of succeeding elsewhere in the world. Switzerland was one of the most difficult and most conservative markets in Europe: 'If we can make it there we can make it anywhere!'[29] The Swiss store opened its doors in 1973 and marked the first step of the company's successful campaign to establish itself in the world. New stores were opened at a furious pace during the following years and IKEA grew into a global home-furnishing chain.

The boy who started off by selling matches was now a mature man and, beyond all the business of home-assembled furniture, thriftiness and a different way of doing things he had discovered something else: 'He had created his own market among people who had never been able to afford new furniture. He had turned to those who lived on very little. Nobody before had ever taken any interest in them.'[30]

In Miriam Salzer's research into the success of IKEA's corporate culture it becomes clear that the creation story helps to establish a 'we' feeling and a collective self-image on the part of the staff: What is it that distinguishes us from others? What makes us different? One way of creating meaning is to retell the story of IKEA's beginnings on the barren soil of Småland and of the young man who created an empire for new colleagues with his bare hands. The glorious past of the story combines with a belief in a fantastic future.[31] The history has not just been used internally, but is also well-known in the wider world where it has been repeated innumerable times, not least in the media. That people seem to love hearing this story is probably because success stories are generally very popular.

There is no infallible recipe for a good story but, for the most part, a number of principle ingredients are included: a message, a conflict, clear roles for the main characters and a plot.[32] In the case of IKEA, the company is presented as though it is permeated by commitment and concern. The moral of the story is that Kamprad is struggling in a headwind to serve the people. His efforts to reduce prices are part of a commitment to society and an ambition to 'create a better everyday life for the many.'

This self-imposed task is regularly repeated in interviews with Kamprad: 'It may sound a little puffed up but I genuinely believe that I have a social mission. For rich people can always do as they please. But I think that everyone else should be able to have a nice home.'[33] Thus it is the company's founder who plays the leading role in the drama and, accordingly, he is described as a kind-hearted man of the people who challenges the establishment. The narrative includes opponents who try to obstruct Kamprad and his noble task. The struggle with the hostile antagonists provides the conflict that generates the forward motion. Besides ill-disposed figures, Kamprad also encounters other adversities but he succeeds in transforming these into opportunities too.

The linear narrative is constructed with a beginning, a middle and an end. Specific events are linked to each other in chronological order with a logical connection and intelligible explanations of IKEA's success concept. The past becomes meaningful while, at the same time, the future is predicted. And the story ends in similar fashion to many other success stories: the hero is victorious, achieving his goal and winning the adulation of the people. Fundamentally this is a remake of Kamprad's testament though in a different genre. The values, visions and attitudes that are explained in the nine theses of the testament are dramatized and remodeled into a captivating story.

The Future is Filled with Possibilities is similar to other narratives of how and why companies are founded. Many of these pertain to the myth of how a man (since it is most usually a man) with his bare hands and a lot of hard work builds an empire or does some mighty deed. If the motivation is a strong commitment and a desire to create something good, the narrative will be all the more powerful.[34] A well-known example of this is the Nike story which tells how runner Phil Knight started the company by selling shoes from the boot of his car. He was driven by a will to win and he saw no obstacles. It was purely a matter of: 'Just do it!'

The narrative promotes Nike's waffle soles as an important step in the company's development and philosophy. When his coach wanted faster shoes for his athletes, Knight began experimenting in his garage with hot rubber. He baked the rubber in a waffle iron and this gave him the famous sole.[35] The narrative is all about the winner mentality. Consumer and athlete are heroes and being beaten is their opponent.

Nike is one of the major brands that has had image problems with revelations about child labor and sweatshop conditions in the third world. The company has coped with this criticism by training staff storytellers, known as Ekins (Nike spelt backwards) whose job is to see to it that all the staff, from middle management to checkout clerks, are aware of the company's roots.[36]

Another famous example is the story of how Steven Wozniak and Steven Jobs became friends at high school and, in due course, built a computer in Jobs' garage: 'Jobs, who had an eye for the future, insisted that he and Wozniak try to sell the machine, and on April 1, 1976, Apple Computer was born.'[37] In spite of the fact that Apple, today, is one of the world's largest and most powerful corporations it still retains a certain rebel image. The two friends who started their business in a garage with their mutual interest in technology but with no money give an impression of not being part of the establishment. True, the story no longer has such a prominent place as formerly, but it still lives on.

The American Ben & Jerry brand also strongly emphasizes its history. The ice-cream company narrates how the two founders, Ben Cohen and Jerry Greenfield, met while still at school thanks to their passion for good food. Following a correspondence course on ice-cream making, the lads started selling ice cream with gigantic bits in and seemingly improbable flavors. Cohen and Greenfield appear as some sort of hippie heroes and the company's image is progressive: 'We're a Company on a mission! . . . Leading with progressive values across our business . . . Love, peace & ice cream.'[38]

The radical image is further strengthened and complemented by the character of the products and the fanciful names. The product is made from natural raw materials and from berries purchased from native Americans. The cherry-flavored ice cream is named after the hippie band Grateful Dead's legendary frontman and guitarist Jerry Garcia and is called 'Cherry Garcia.'[39] In 2000 Ben & Jerry was sold to multinational Unilever, one of the world's biggest manufacturers of staple foods, and a corporation which certainly does not have the same image as the original owners. But the narrative has not changed. Unilever has clearly not just purchased the company but also the concept and the story of Ben & Jerry.

That the rebel image is attractive and thus commercially advantageous is one of the theses in Heath and Potter's book The Rebel Sell: How the Counterculture Became Consumer Culture (2005) which has a strikingly appropriate image on the cover: a latte mug with a picture of Che Guevara. The thesis of the book is that, ultimately, anti-consumerism is only another form of consumerism. A nicely packaged form of anti-capitalism that can give an aura of iconoclasm but that is actually status-seeking and snobbish.[40]

There is also a rebel theme to IKEA's story. This portrays the company as breaking with accepted conventions and thus appearing to be oppositional. Kamprad the hero is not just hindered by malicious antagonists but he also courageously defies the hidebound furniture industry and thus revolutionizes it. The company's narrative activities are not, thus, unique, but there are few other examples in which the story so permeates the corporate culture and resonates so strongly with the consumer.

The 'IKEA Way': what and how to do it

The Future is Filled with Possibilities does not just portray IKEA's journey from a being a small-scale rebel to becoming an established international chain of furniture stores. Like many fables it is equipped with a moral. By following its own path—'The IKEA Way'—IKEA became successful. Hand in hand with Kamprad's testament the narrative has acted as a moral guide as to how the staff should act and how they should deal with

27

Challenge

Having passed the checkouts, most visitors were tired, hungry and grumpy. Sometimes people were getting a bad last impression of the IKEA store. Maybe they had to wait in line at the check outs. Or maybe we had run out of a product they wanted to buy.

Solution

To create a positive, lasting impression and to send a dramatic low-price message, we took the bold decision to sell hot dogs for just SEK 5 in the exit area. This was an incredible price compared to the normal price on the market of SEK 15 to 20. Today we apply the same principle all over the world. It is not always a hot dog. In Italy it is pizza, for example. Then we applied the same thinking to our product range. What would happen if we could offer a well-known product on the market for a price that would amaze people? The idea of the "hot dog" product was born.

© Inter IKEA Systems B.V. 2010

Inter IKEA Systems B.V. **IKEA**

Figure 2.3 Postcard from the Inter IKEA Cultural Center, Älmhult. (Used with the permission of Inter IKEA Systems B.V. © Inter IKEA Systems B.V.)

problems.[41] *The Testament of a Furniture Dealer* and *The Future is Filled with Possibilities* act as sources from which one can fetch and focus on episodes and parts. Buried among the anecdotes, stories and fables there are directives, norms and values. Thus the two texts function as management tools.

In the interactive display at IKEA's corporate center there are numerous postcards (Figure 2.3) devoted to fragments of the narrative, including the challenges and problems that Kamprad and the company have faced in the past and how they have dealt with them: 'Challenge: Ingvar Kamprad started buying boxes of matches for 1.5 Swedish pennies a box. He sold them for 5 cents, but this was too expensive for the thrifty customers of Småland. Solution: He went to Stockholm where he could buy boxes of matches for almost half the price. He learned that his customers benefited when he acted as a middleman to find better sources of purchasing.'[42]

During the 1980s the original narrative was transformed into a sort of management language. IKEA formulated its corporate culture and defined the brand identity in a more strategic way than in the past. They became more aware of the value of the corporate culture and the importance of looking after it. In turn, the corporate culture can not only be perceived in the narratives but also in rituals, ceremonies, manners, behavior and dress. Nowadays there are numerous workplaces in the corporate sector where staff do not have to wear ties or even jackets. But at IKEA dress has always been informal and fairly casual.[43]

In the 1980s the testament was refined into a concept expressed in a manual which resulted in numerous documents dealing with the corporate culture and the brand as well as direct instructions about the operation.[44] The numerous manuals were accompanied by an extensive program of training with courses such as 'Discovering the IKEA Concept,' 'IKEA Staff Planning,' 'IKEA Swedish Food Market' and 'IKEA Sales and Range Management.'[45]

Naturally the corporate culture is not completely uniform, varying somewhat from place to place.[46] The point of these manuals and the training schemes is to implement and strengthen the overall value system. But there are also legal reasons for their existence. IKEA has sought to protect its brand using documents in which the concept and the operations are defined. One reason for the growing number of manuals was a dispute

Figure 2.4 Opening the new store in Älmhult, November 2012. Instead of the usual procedure of cutting a ribbon, IKEA has chosen, ever since the 1970s, to saw through a log. (Used with the permission of Inter IKEA Systems B.V. © Inter IKEA Systems B.V.)

with the American company STøR Furnishings International Inc. that IKEA sued in 1987 for employing a very similar concept.

According to IKEA, their competitor had basically copied their concept straight off. The stores and the catalogs had been plagiarized down to the smallest details.[47] But the American company had not succeeded in copying IKEA's corporate culture which is generally considered to be an important key to the company's success. IKEA describes it as a tool for realizing the visions contained in the testament but it is also a way of communicating the company's identity to the customers.[48] One of many ways in which IKEA manifests its uniqueness is in the way that it celebrates the opening of a new store. Instead of the usual procedure of cutting a ribbon, IKEA has chosen, ever since the 1970s, to saw through a log. The action is intended to indicate that IKEA breaks with traditions and does things differently (Figure 2.4).[49] That the company has chosen a log is no accident either since a large proportion of the product range consists of items made of wood.

Language is another important aspect of IKEA's corporate culture. It should be easily comprehensible and unbureaucratic. Work at IKEA should be based on enthusiasm, a constant desire for renewal and for taking responsibility, cost-consciousness, humility with regard to one's tasks, and modest behavior.[50] Each year there are 'anti-bureaucracy weeks' in which staff who do not normally come into contact with the customers are able to work on the floor of the store.[51] In other words, even senior managers should understand what it is like to work in the warehouse or at the checkout. Staff are expected to use only first names regardless of their position in the company: 'A job well executed at IKEA earns a person more respect than a glamorous title. . . .'[52]

It is true that IKEA does not work with traditional status symbols that signal hierarchy and that the company prides itself on having a fairly flat organization in which people behave informally and titles are not important. But this does not mean that there is no management structure. The hierarchical divisions between managers and people working 'on the floor' are expressed in more subtle ways.[53] That the IKEA spirit as described in the manuals is not just empty rhetoric but has been used as a method of solving actual problems is evident from an internal project entitled Kraft–80 which was also responsible for generating the idea of the 'anti-bureaucracy weeks.'[54]

The plan was initiated against the background of some actual problems that arose as a result of IKEA's rapid expansion. In a message to the staff, Kamprad opined that what was needed was 'several thousand kilos of brain in a year-long internal operation for meeting the 1980s. We need to learn to listen more closely to each and every one of our colleagues. All ideas should be followed up and carefully evaluated. We need to fight against the spread of bureaucracy in the group. We shall seriously reward good ideas in different fields . . . The final goal of Kraft–80 is a new IKEA—better equipped for the year 2000.'[55]

Kraft–80 was, quite simply, a sort of wide-ranging critical survey and refining of a somewhat confused operation that had developed growing pains. There were missing nuts, legs that broke and designs that were structurally unsound. Staff lacked rules and guidelines. At Älmhult IKEA created a power center—the so-called 'Kraftcentralen'—and a newsletter entitled 'IKEA Match' presented historic flashbacks, evaluations, reports, reportage and interviews with staff members.[56] New issues of 'IKEA Match' appeared frequently and regularly and they indicate that the program was a collective project with solidarity and partnership at the center.

Many of the newsletters dealt with practical problems that the company was struggling with. Staff lacked information and clear rules: What was one to do when there was no more of a product in the warehouse? How were products to be presented? And how were staff to deal with angry customers?[57] 'Kraft–80' can also be seen as an implementation of Kamprad's vision as expressed in his testament. The project produced concrete ideas and sales strategies that were further developed in due course and made available in written form. The project was followed by several internal campaigns.[58]

In parallel with producing instructions, the brand and the corporate culture were defined in manuals. The company distinguishes between 'IKEA values' and 'brand values.' While 'IKEA values' are concerned with the norms that should permeate the company internally, 'brand values' are about how one wants the brand to be perceived around the world.[59] In spite of this division there are obvious links between the two categories, or in IKEA's own words: 'Understanding and being familiar with the IKEA culture is essential in order to fully operate the IKEA concept in practice.'[60] Since the end of the 1990s, ten key expressions have summarized the IKEA culture:

- Leadership by example
- Simplicity

- Striving to meet reality

- Constantly being 'on the way'

- Cost-consciousness

- Constant desire for renewal

- Humbleness and willpower

- Daring to be different

- Togetherness and enthusiasm

- Accept and delegate responsibility.[61]

These key expressions are really just a reformulation of values taken from *The Testament of a Furniture Dealer* and *A Little IKEA Dictionary*, and they are described in more detail in *IKEA Concept Description* (2000). The manual has the appropriate nickname of 'The mother of all manuals' and it is a wide-ranging account of the main aspects of the concept and how they interact.[62] As well as the business strategy and corporate culture already described, the stores themselves and the catalog are also highly significant.[63] The catalog is one of IKEA's strongest cards. It is the world's largest circulation printed publication at close to 200 million copies in twenty-seven languages. It consists mainly of pictures of homes and people using the furniture and household utensils with the prices clearly stated.[64] Until the mid-1960s the focus of the catalog was on the products as such, but as the company began to stage interiors and everyday settings in the stores, these found their way into the catalog as well.[65] The images are documentary in character, unpretentious and with a strong sense of presence. The mood has always been jauntily familiar and inclusive: We understand your situation and we are here to help you. Initially Kamprad wrote the texts himself and the familiar tone was his own. By the 2010s there were some ten staff copywriters and the company still emphasizes the importance of maintaining an unpretentious approach though they claim that 'it takes several years to learn the style, to break the code of what to sound like.'[66]

The aim of the catalog is to express and confirm the brand identity and, especially, to attract customers to the stores. In turn, the stores are expected to function as effective selling machines, giving inspiration and offering expertise in interior design as well as providing a fun excursion for the whole family. The overall goal is to transform visitors into customers and to persuade them to buy as much as possible. You may have entered the store with the intention of buying a sofa but IKEA's aim is that, the moment you have crossed the threshold, you should catch sight of all sorts of other things that you did not previously know you needed: 'stimulate visitors to make impulse purchases by bringing to their attention needs that they were unaware of before they entered the store. . . .'[67]

The testament also resounds in *Our Way. The Brand Values Behind the IKEA Concept* which was published in the early 1990s and which maps IKEA's specific identity.[68] Defining what the brand is all about is just as much a question of noting what it is not about. Using contrasts in words and images, IKEA pinpoints the values of its own brand. The opponent acts as a mirror or reference point for emphasizing the difference.

The contrasts were illustrated with appropriate photographs: 'Functional—Not fancy' was exemplified by two wristwatches, one of them extremely simple with a black strap and white dial while the other was richly decorated with diamonds and gold (Plate 1). Equally educational was the illustration dedicated to 'Smart and thrifty—Not extravagant': IKEA's famous short, plain pencils are shown alongside Mont Blanc. Equally significant are the cheap hotdogs that are on sale in the stores which are compared with a jar of caviar: 'For the many—Not for the few.' Other values and pairs of opposites are: 'Clear—Not complicated, Honest—Not Fake, Light-hearted—Not dull, Passionate—Not indifferent, Surprising—Not expected, Warm and human—Not cold and distant, Inexpensive—Not expensive, Rebellious—Not conformist, Swedish—Not from anywhere.'[69]

The year 2011 saw IKEA's values updated and reduced in number from twelve to five: 'Honesty, Affordability, Solutions, Inspiration, Surprises.'[70] The new variants, which are also basic to the internal staff-training strategy, are intended to be easier to understand, not least on account of numerous different cultures in which they have to function.[71] While the manuals already described categorize the brand and the corporate culture, there are other, more tangible instructions pertaining to IKEA's many different operational areas including creating displays, the warehouses and the restaurants.

A central theme of the manuals is the pick-it-up-yourself philosophy, so-called mechanical selling which requires customers to find articles themselves, and to pick them up from the store (Figure 2.5). This refers to all items that do not need to be sold by trained staff but can be effectuated with the help of the catalog, clearly marked prices and other information on display. But sophisticated methods are essential if this sales strategy is to prove successful. Every now and then IKEA uses so-called 'commercial reviews' to check that the stores are following directives. These reviews monitor a number of obligatory directives, awarding points.[72]

Manuals about techniques of presentation well illustrate how detailed the directives and instructions about operational matters actually are. Over the years, what Kamprad has described as 'seduction activities' have been developed and adapted into detailed instructions about how the flow of customers should be led through the store, what interiors must be exhibited and how the products are to be displayed.[73] That these rules aim to increase sales is no secret. On the contrary, this ambition is explicit: 'Almost 100% of all IKEA customers buy more than they had originally planned. A result of effective range presentation.'[74]

It is, of course, no accident that the first thing visitors to the stores encounter at the entrance is a mountain of yellow and blue shopping bags. The design was introduced at the end of the 1980s: 'The real challenge is to introduce the yellow bag as quickly as possible . . . to ensure that every customer or family has a yellow bag thrust upon them right from the start. . . .'[75] The idea is, accordingly, that at the same moment a customer takes a bag she or he has set the purchasing process in motion.

The manual intimates that IKEA holds hands with the customers all the way from the entrance to the checkout. There are few straight passages and these are short. At each turn of the route the customer is presented with new products at various price levels strategically placed in room displays, on shelves, in boxes, or piled up in heaps. The idea of the realistic interiors is to illustrate different styles and tastes. The intention is not that

Figure 2.5 Ballerup, Denmark, probably 1969. (Used with the permission of Inter IKEA Systems B.V. © Inter IKEA Systems B.V.)

the customer should buy the entire room but, rather, that the products should be presented in an attractive context which stimulates consumption. The room displays provide an effective sales tool. If we cannot afford the table in the room we can at least buy the vase that is displayed on it as a consolation prize. Vases are strategically placed on a shelf or a tray next to the room display.

On the customer's way out of one particular department and in to the next one there is a 'closing offer': 'one last opportunity to buy one or more products before leaving one speciality shop and entering the next.'[76] The cheapest products of all are displayed at regular points throughout the store. The idea is that the price should be so modest that the products become almost irresistible. This category of products is known as 'open-the-wallet' or 'breath-taking-item' and is usually presented using the 'bulla-bulla' method: 'The bulla-bulla display technique uses a large stock of the same product to create product dominance. This sends a clear low-price message and stimulates impulse buying . . .'[77] These special offers tempt customers right up to the checkout: 'the final opportunity for selling impulse products.'[78]

That IKEA, in company with other commercial undertakings, should employ a variety of strategies with a view to maximizing sales is not surprising. But one can hardly avoid being struck by the discrepancies exhibited by the messages contained in the different manuals. In some of the manuals that define the corporate culture and the brand the emphasis is on the idea that the organization is driven by a vision of creating a better everyday life for the common man and that this is characterized by social concerns: 'At IKEA it is not just a matter of earning money or of expanding just for the sake of growth. Our task is to make life a little better for the broad mass of people.'[79] Other manuals are concerned with encouraging people to buy as much as possible: 'Help visitors buy, and they will buy more.'[80]

I'm your man

At the core of IKEA's mythology is the figure of Ingvar Kamprad himself (Plate 2). Stories about what he has said and done are central elements and they have acted as a guide for the staff like good examples of people with power. If his testament represents the manifesto, then the man himself is the model. But the stories have even spread outside the organization as such, where Kamprad has featured in IKEA's advertising. Regardless of whether the characteristics of his personality are genuine or fictitious, they certainly express the brand. Some of the stories can be dismissed as being just too improbable, but this does not seem to matter. The mythology seems to be stronger than reality itself. The stories testify to and strengthen what IKEA stands for and believes in.

The innumerable interviews with Kamprad and the portraits of him are all much the same. Generally speaking he gives the same replies, sounding like standardized answers or an IKEA mantra. The stories resonate within the organization and beyond like the chorus of a song. Over and over again the image of a down-to-earth, modest and charmingly unassuming entrepreneur is drummed in. He is generally portrayed as unbelievably thrifty, jovial, friendly and folksy. The man who set out empty-handed and built an empire, but who kept his feet on the ground and maintained contact with his staff. It is claimed that he never flies business class or stays in luxury hotels, preferring public transport rather than a company car and replacing the bottle of soda water from his hotel minibar with a bottle purchased the next day in the local convenience store. It is claimed that he looks out for special offers and that he prefers to take a hotdog at an IKEA store for his lunch rather than eating in the restaurant.[81]

Kamprad's legendary frugality and extreme friendliness are both concrete and symbolic. It is entirely possible that the founder of IKEA counts his change and lives in much the same style as Swedes in general. But regardless of whether he is thrifty, and if so exactly how thrifty he is, the image has been important to IKEA. The founder's characteristics express and communicate the corporate culture and the brand.[82]

Kamprad has succeeded in retaining the image of a distinctly ordinary person. But at the same time that he describes himself as intellectually flawed, suffering from limitations in his ability to read and write, as well as being shy and fond of alcohol, Kamprad has, *de facto*, created one of the world's most successful companies. In Sweden he is regarded as something of a national hero. And despite the fact that both he and the company have met with serious criticism over the years, both he and IKEA enjoy a high level of trust. In 2008, for example, IKEA came top of the list in a survey of which institutions in society Swedes trusted most.[83] Trust in IKEA was, for example, greater than trust in the Swedish parliament or the Swedish Church.

Portraits of Kamprad constantly underline various characteristics: 'His total lack of outward show, exclusive clothes and habits, expensive watches, smart cars (he drives an old Volvo estate car) . . . On one of his birthdays he could not decide whether to buy some wine: Most of the guests will bring a bottle, he opined . . . On checking our diaries one day we canceled a meeting because IK [Ingvar Kamprad] had to use up his SAS [Scandinavian Airlines] bonus points before that . . .'[84]

Kamprad likes to tell people about his modest habits: 'If I had fun with my money. The answer is that I have been too frugal. My wife once suggested to me that I might buy her just one thing that was not bought in a sale.'[85] 'I still visit street markets. I wait until they are just packing up and then ask if I can buy something a little more cheaply. My wife is rather tired of me.'[86] Or: 'I am dyslexic, tone deaf and I love visiting hypermarkets.'[87]

Many of IKEA's sales techniques and ideas derive from Kamprad's frugality. A notable example is the story of how the short, plain pencils available in the stores originated and why they are like they are. Kamprad wanted pencils to be available in the stores and he asked one of his buyers to solve the problem: 'But they must naturally be cheap pencils' he added. When he met up again with the buyer to view the alternatives Kamprad asked: 'What are the pencils like?' The buyer answered: 'Here you are' and placed a pencil on the desk. 'But why does it look like this?' Kamprad asked. 'What do you mean? It's a standard Swedish pencil.' Kamprad objected: 'Yes, but why does it need to be so long? And why should it be yellow or green?' The buyer explained: 'This is what pencils look like. It's the Swedish standard.' Kamprad picked up the pencil and broke it into two pieces. 'Now we have two pencils for the same price. They're equally good for writing with. And suppose we take away the yellow paint. We don't need that. Now we have IKEA standard.'[88]

Kamprad's capacity for doing things differently—which is best portrayed in *The Future is Filled with Possibilities*—is backed up by a succession of stories about him in which the moral of the tale is precisely originality and innovation. There is a story about Kamprad leaning over the frozen foods in a supermarket, eagerly holding up a frozen duck and asking one of the staff: 'Can you see what it says?' The employee answered, surprised: 'It's a duck,' and received the answer: 'I know it's a duck, but can you see what it says? Product of Romania . . . what do they do with all the feathers?'[89] It is a matter of being able to see the business opportunities in every situation.

Besides being frugal and modest Kamprad appears as a folk hero with human weaknesses and shortcomings. Unlike many other international businessmen Kamprad presents a relatively unsophisticated and modest exterior: he dresses unassumingly, uses

Swedish snuff, smiles in a friendly manner and talks in a strong dialect from his native Småland or in shaky English about how ordinary and simple he is: 'I am a typical Swede. I'm only happy if I have a glass of schnapps.'[90]

Kamprad reveals his human side by speaking openly about his problems with alcohol and dyslexia as well as his lack of formal education: 'Hell, if I could only be a bit cultural, like my wife who can read novels . . . My absolute limit is picking up catalogs to leaf through . . . the books that I have really read right to the end can be numbered on the fingers of one hand.'[91] Having the common touch is not the same thing as being uneducated. But the fact that Kamprad constantly stresses his intellectual limitations lines up with his image as an unpretentious person and from there it is not a giant step to devaluing higher education altogether: 'What does he want with a fancy degree if he is working with us.'[92]

A university education and imposing titles are considered as snobbish attributes: 'Just as fancy titles do little to help the image of IKEA as an unconventional concept. Of course, we want our key people to become well-known—but more for what they do than because of their business cards.'[93] The message is that Kamprad certainly does not believe himself to be superior to anyone else, but it also tells us something about the organization: 'Taking responsibility has nothing to do with education, financial position or rank. Responsibility-takers can be found in the warehouse.'[94]

Kamprad describes himself as more of a philanthropist interested in building society rather than merely a businessman: 'What keeps me going is a sense of taking part in a gigantic democratization project. . . .'[95] There is constant mention of social pathos: 'I asked myself [in the 1950s] why poor people had to put up with ugly products. Did it have to be the case that beautiful things could only be bought at great expense by an elite in society?'[96] Kamprad also presents himself as a sort of beneficent capitalist: 'I have always disliked the hard-headed American type of jungle capitalism and I must confess to having certain socialist sympathies . . . As a young man I was fascinated by the brilliance of Ernst Wigforss [Swedish social democrat and Finance Minister] and his reflections on how the wealth of the nation could be justly shared.'[97]

As we have noted, Kamprad's difficulties with reading and writing are frequently emphasized. At times there are contradictory references to his reading socially committed authors. 'I read quite a bit, for example about Karin and Carl Larsson [artists] and Ellen Key [social critic and feminist].'[98]

There are other voices that portray Kamprad as a man of the people too: 'Sweden. The wintry little European country that didn't hesitate to raise their collective voice in the 1960s and 70s (under Prime Minister Olof Palme) when it came to injustice and inequity in the world. In some ways, IKEA is a child of that same spirit—an activist. With Ingvar Kamprad in the role of underdog . . . he is quick in both his public speaking and catalogs to take the side of the average person against the powerful economic establishment.'[99]

Kamprad is IKEA's hero and is an excellent example of the fact that the image of the founder of a business is often of great importance to the brand. But a simple background is not necessarily part of a branding exercise. Unlike Kamprad, fashion designer Ralph Lauren does not claim simple origins; quite the reverse. Though he was born Ralph Lifshitz in the poor Bronx district of New York in 1939 he is generally portrayed in an

Figure 2.6 Ingvar Kamprad, outside the first store in Älmhult, 1960s. (Used with the permission of Inter IKEA Systems B.V. © Inter IKEA Systems B.V.)

upper-class luster. And the history of the Ralph Lauren brand including the Polo trademark has largely been created through the consistent use of a specific pictorial image: beautiful young people enjoying a leisurely and luxurious time on a yacht or playing polo.

Nowadays the pictorial image is so established that it hardly needs the actual trademark for us to recognize the distinct style. The same is true of Estée Lauder who grew up in very modest circumstances in New York with the name Josephine Esther Mentzer. During the 1930s she succeeded in building a brand that is associated with European luxury and glamour.[100]

In retrospect Kamprad's emblem seems to have been crafted in tune with the development of the corporate culture and the brand. In photographs from the 1960s, Kamprad can be seen wearing a business suit and owned a Porsche (Figure 2.6).[101] But during the 1970s Kamprad changed his image from strict businessman to one of the lads on the floor wearing jeans and a shirt with the sleeves rolled up and with a pinch of Swedish snuff under his lip. Times and fashions change, of course, but in this context it is interesting that Kamprad's image changed as IKEA's own profile and corporate culture developed.

There is much to suggest that Kamprad has become what he now is. It is also probable that he lives in accordance with his precepts; that is that he actually does hunt for bargains, travels on budget airlines and never stays in luxury hotels. It is just as probable that Kamprad is modest, friendly and a man of the people. But few people seem to realize that staying in cheaper hotels and not traveling first class are part of his job. For the benefit of the company he maintains an image that fits with the company's needs. Kamprad represents the brand and he has gradually achieved a branded persona, a sort of IKEA's Ronald McDonald.

Thus the founder's official image raises interesting questions about the connection between a persona and the brand. To put it another way: to what extent has Kamprad been influenced by his own idea? To what extent has the IKEA brand shaped him and to what extent has Kamprad shaped IKEA? Perhaps one can view Kamprad's image as an unusually successful manifestation. The simple, man-of-the-people image seems to be part of the business idea with his own image being part of the concept.

Different ways of narrating IKEA

Miriam Salzer's research on the internal corporate culture at IKEA reveals that the narratives are, to a great extent, part of an oral tradition. Anecdotes, stories and fables were formerly not available in written policies or manuals but were handed down among the staff.[102] But over the years numerous stories have been published inside the company. By 2013 there were more than a thousand stories available on the company intranet. These had been collected from staff members and divided into categories: 'IKEA Values, IKEA Concept, [Store] Area, New Markets and other cultures, IKEA Co-workers.'[103]

In earlier times storytelling seems to have been more spontaneous and less organized, but has since become formalized and used internally. A selection of the collected narratives has even been published on DVD, and in books and pamphlets. The stories consist mainly of memories and experiences as to how people at IKEA have solved problems or have arrived at new ideas.[104] There is no direct link to *The Testament of a Furniture Dealer* but the narratives can definitely be likened to 'theory in practice.' Quite simply, they illustrate the values, dogmas and spirit that pervade the testament.

The book *10 Years of Stories from IKEA People* (2008) is a collection of narratives from staff in China. The overall motto of creating a better everyday life for people is constantly repeated or stated in different words. Several stories deal with just how fantastic IKEA is and the ways in which it has changed the authors' lives: 'I am lucky that I am a member of the big IKEA family! . . . I firmly believe that I will always live this happily, just like how I approve of the IKEA management philosophy and cultural values!'[105]

One of the narratives in *IKEA Stories* (Figure 2.7) illustrates the norms of simplicity, modesty and equality: 'When I was interviewed for my IKEA job I wore a tie. I think I got the job despite the tie. Certainly not because of it.'[106] This member of staff goes on to explain that the man who interviewed him later regularly looked in on him to ask: 'Hey, how's it going today' or 'Wanna go for lunch?' The new employee realized in due course that the friendly and modest colleague actually had a very senior position in the company: 'A big league player. And I was just . . . I was astonished. Because, like I say, from the corporate culture that I knew, this guy wouldn't have the first idea what my first name was.'[107]

Another narrative emphasizes team spirit and solidarity. The employee remembers how she explained a critical situation to her boss: 'I'm not kidding you, I had seven

Figure 2.7 DVD, 'IKEA Stories.' The stories consist mainly of stories and experiences as to how people at IKEA have solved problems or have arrived at new ideas and illustrate the values, dogmas and spirit that pervade *The Testament of a Furniture Dealer*. (Used with the permission of Inter IKEA Systems B.V. © Inter IKEA Systems B.V.)

managers putting up their hands straightaway. "I'll be there, Laurie!" they said. "You need this, I'll be there. No problem!" . . . That taught me at a very early stage that in the IKEA organization there will always be people to help you out.'[108] The moral of the tale is that IKEA's employees help each other out, including senior management.

Another story illustrates the notion that one can learn from mistakes and that staff should not be afraid of making mistakes. One man remembers how, as a new employee, he managed to shut off the electricity to the lighting department in the store. Instead of being castigated by his colleagues they remarked, enthusiastically: 'So now you've learnt something!'[109] Several narratives deal with methods of selling and with products. Best known is the episode about how the flat packages came about. According to IKEA the idea turned up in a flash in the 1950s when an employee was unable to get a table into the boot of a car: 'Exploration of flat packaging begins when one of the first IKEA co-workers removes the legs of the LÖVET table so that it will fit into a car and avoid damage during transit. After this discovery flat packs and self-assembly become part of the concept' (Figure 2.8).[110]

According to one employee, displaying products in large stacks or piles to signal a bargain was inspired by his childhood: 'I'm one of eleven children, so my poor mother never knew for certain how many of her children she would be catering for on any given weekend. Instead she used to spend ages preparing what we would nowadays call "buffet meals." She'd pile up huge quantities of appetizing little nibbles. . . . It was this idea of Mum's that we translated more or less directly into a sales display technique.'[111]

One piece of furniture that IKEA has paid special attention to is the 'Billy' bookcase which, in 2009, was honored with a book written as though describing a person (Figure 2.9).[112] The text starts with a brief interview in which Billy answers questions about personal data, zodiac sign, family, strengths and weaknesses and the bookcases he is most satisfied with or does not like. One spread is devoted to the narrower bookshelf called 'Benno' which is designed for storing compact discs and films and which is Billy's best friend. 'We complement each other perfectly, though I say it myself. I like books. While BENNO is more for films and music . . . He's a real film buff.'[113]

Billy's girlfriend is 'Bergsbo' which is a wider type of shelving: 'What brought us together was, of course, our passion for books and I think we match each other admirably. I look after the smaller ones and she deals with the larger ones.'[114] The book traces Billy's life from its birth in 1979 until the year 2009 with references to political and social changes as well as developments in popular culture. For example, the book notes that in the year that 'Billy' was born rock band The Clash released their album 'London Calling,' and 'Billy' started being manufactured in birch veneer exactly 50 years after the conclusion of World War II. There is a section devoted to the name of the product, and numerous famous people who share the name are listed including actor Billy Crystal and performer Billy Joel. IKEA's 'Billy' also shares favorite sandwich recipes with us and suggests books to interest adults and children.

In the real world there is no natural connection between sandwich recipes, The Clash, Billy Crystal and the 'Billy' bookshelf, but the book represents a way of dramatizing the rather dry factual information about year of manufacture, materials and production methods. Stories about specific IKEA products are not uncommon, nor is IKEA unique in this. In the beauty industry, for example, there are innumerable tales about miracle

Figure 2.8 'Lövet' [Leaf], mid-1950s. (Used with the permission of Inter IKEA Systems B.V. © Inter IKEA Systems B.V.)

Figure 2.9 *BILLY*, 2009. (Used with the permission of Inter IKEA Systems B.V. © Inter IKEA Systems B.V.)

ointments and secret recipes. These tales become a significant part of the success of the product and, despite the fact that the degree of truth is highly doubtful, the narratives prove useful. The physical ingredients represent a tiny fraction of the price. Success is concerned, rather, with how the product is launched, the symbols and design, and the promises that we can be transformed into better and more attractive versions of ourselves.

A well-known story that has been related by beauty journalists, sales staff and consumers alike focuses on how skin-care company Elizabeth Arden's 'Eight Hour Cream' was created. It was claimed that Arden's horse had sustained a nasty wound in a riding accident and that no pharmaceuticals seemed able to cure it. Arden asked her chemists to produce an ointment that would heal the wound. She then started using the ointment herself. The recipe is secret.[115]

There is a similar story about 'Crème de la Mer.' In parallel with Arden's horse, an engineer at NASA was involved in an accident with rocket fuel. While struggling to heal his skin he made a sensational discovery: if one collected a certain type of seaweed at just the right time of the month and let the seaweed ferment for four months it developed a highly curative effect. Using the almost magical algae the engineer produced a miraculous ointment that saved his skin: 'Crème de la Mer.'[116]

The narratives about the ointments are basically disseminated orally. For IKEA, too, the oral tradition has been important and passing on narratives within the company must be considered against a background of the concept of 'word-of-mouth' as oral communication of stories is known in marketing. When a consumer tells someone about a specific product or brand this gives the story a more credible impression than the usual sort of advertising since the situation is not a commercial one. If the story is positive about the product the consumer becomes a sort of unpaid ambassador or advertising hoarding for the brand. The story may have been planted at the behest of the company but can also have arisen spontaneously.[117]

Coca-Cola Light, to take an example, long suffered from a persistent rumor that the drink contained dangerous substances. The tales can be likened to popular modern fables that reveal our secret dreams and anxieties. Ironically, Coca-Cola is a company that involved consumers in the corporate narrative from an early stage in order to promote credibility. Consumers contribute to the corporate narrative and they are transformed into a sort of advertising hoarding. Over the years Coca-Cola has collected 'true stories' about what the brand has meant to people's lives from all over the world: how it has affected them in love, friendship and war.[118]

Customers' narratives are, nowadays, not just transmitted orally but are communicated on websites as well as in books and films. One example from IKEA is a book about people's memories of furniture, which was published in connection with the fiftieth anniversary (2008) of the first IKEA store in Älmhult.[119] Side by side with stories from customers there is information about the social structure of Sweden in the 1950s. Customers are integrated into the company's narrative with their personal descriptions of helpful sales staff and the delights of making purchases. The anecdotes create a sense of authenticity and the generalized information about society acts as a meaningful framework.

'Not for the rich. But for the wise'

Stories about IKEA that have been disseminated and retold by customers and the media have been important to brand reception, but external and strategic communication has been just as important. In this context, too, the Brindfors agency had a decisive influence. The agency staff made an important contribution in formulating and building the brand, not least with the creation story published as *The Future is Filled with Possibilities*. Brindfors also played a central role in external marketing which helped to establish the mythology surrounding IKEA. As the chain of stores developed in Europe, the Brindfors agency became increasingly international, opening a branch in Germany, for example, in order to meet IKEA's needs in establishing itself in other markets.[120]

Just as with other parts of the company, IKEA's communications are directed by guidelines about everything from how the logotype is to be used and how big events should be planned.[121] Advertising is mainly created locally and instructions can be interpreted in different ways in different countries, but the final result is controlled by Inter IKEA Systems.[122] Marketing strategies differ from country to country but, generally speaking, IKEA's advertising has been perceived as being cheeky, clever and humorous and, not least, challenging and provocative.

When IKEA established itself in the USA in 1985 the company big-headedly opined: 'It's a Big Country. Someone's Got to Furnish It.' In the UK the challenge was to 'Chuck Out Your Chintz' (1996) in a campaign which was followed, for example, by 'Stop Being So English' (2000). Another memorable example is 'Embrace Change 09,' a sort of tribute to Barack Obama's accession to the presidency in 2009 (Plate 3). The advertising included a replica of the Oval Office displayed at Union Station in Washington DC furnished with items from IKEA; as well as advertisements with messages like 'Change Begins at Home' and 'The Time for Domestic Reform is Now!'

The tone was set by the Brindfors agency which established a strategy during the 1980s, thus helping to lay the foundations for the company's external communication. Collaboration with IKEA started with the rapid growth of the company which led to an increased need to shape the company's identity. The collaboration continued until the late 1990s and it embraced a large number of countries.[123] This period witnessed the production of innumerable advertisements and campaigns, designed by Brindfors, which can be basically understood as a Swedish version of the so-called creative revolution within the advertising industry that started in and spread from New York.[124]

This revolution in the advertising industry is generally associated with Bill Bernbach who had questioned the industry's strategies back in the 1940s, and who is accepted as the leading light of the movement. Formerly the commercial message had generally been communicated through didactic, humorless advertisements replete with factual information. But consumers were deafened by unique offers from all directions and it became increasingly difficult for companies to make their voices heard.

Bernbach maintained that the nagging and officious tone of advertisements meant that people avoided them, choosing to look in a different direction or shutting their ears. If one wanted to gain people's attention one needed to converse with them instead of speaking at them. It was not just a matter of what was to be said, but how it was said. According to Bernbach, the solution was creativity and artistry. An important factor was that the creative aspect in designing advertising campaigns was given much more space than in the past. It was now a matter of coming up with ideas rather than following a traditional book of rules and this led on to new methods of working. Instead of a strict division of labor, copywriters and artistic designers worked together, resulting in a collective approach that generated more and better ideas.

One highly illustrative example is the DDB agency's famous advertisements for Volkswagen. Their assignment was seemingly impossible: in a country where a large car spells status, to launch a small, rather ridiculous and totally unglamorous motor car that had originally been favored by Hitler. The solution was to produce advertisements that were the very opposite of conventional motorcar ads. Rather than photographing the car in an exclusive setting, in front of a suburban house or in the company of an attractive woman, the 'Beetle' was launched using naked, black and white photography with an equally plain and impersonal graphic design.[125] There was an advertisement featuring the expression 'Lemon' (meaning pretty useless) in bold letters, though it did not address the car's limitations; quite the reverse. According to the message, the car shown in the ad had been rejected by Volkswagen because there was a scratch on its paintwork. If, instead, the advertisement had soberly claimed that the manufacturer carried out rigorous quality controls the ad would hardly have created the same impression.

The trend now was to use a smart type of humor as a selling point by suggesting that the German quality controllers were somewhat neurotic perfectionists. And, rather than repeating the same advertisement innumerable times, the DBB agency pumped out new variants. Another of the Volkswagen ads shows the car in front of a house, conveying the message: 'It Makes Your House Look Bigger.' A third poster shows the car with a police badge on the door with a text that reads: 'Don't Laugh.'[126]

This creative revolution spread throughout the western world like rings on water and Brindfors was one of the Swedish agencies that drew inspiration from the American precursors.[127] There were times when advertisements for IKEA were very close to the American originals, for example in Paul Rand's advertisements. The American graphic designer, who had created legendary logotypes for IBM, ABC television and Westinghouse, often caught people's attention by leaving some space for the beholder's own imagination. A poster from 1982 transformed the IBM logo into a picture puzzle or rebus: an eye, a bee and the M from the actual logotype: 'Eye-Bee-M.'[128] Three years later, when the first US IKEA store was to open in Philadelphia, the company clearly borrowed Rand's idea. The IKEA ad was concerned with teaching customers to pronounce IKEA correctly and was presented as a rebus: an eye, a key, and the exclamation 'ah': IKEA (Figure 2.10).[129]

Robin Hood of the furniture industry: from the high street to the Masses

When IKEA became one of Brindfors' clients, the furniture chain was relatively well-known throughout Sweden, particularly for its bargain prices. But the company also struggled with something of a poor reputation. People were aware that the furniture was cheap to buy. But few people associated IKEA with quality.[130] The advertising agency's task was to give the brand a more positive tone and they achieved this using clever, witty, and often ironical slogans that caught people's attention and provoked their interest.[131]

Brindfors' first assignment for IKEA was to launch the refurbished flagship store at Kungens Kurva on the outskirts of Stockholm. The building had been subjected to a major refit and, two weeks before the doors opened to the public again, there were exhortations on hoardings like 'Make sure you're not broke on 25, 26, 27 or 28 October. A whole new IKEA is opening with thousands of bargains!!!,' 'Take a day off . . .,' 'Don't go on holiday . . .,' 'Don't be ill. . . .'

A few days before the opening there were further warnings: 'Cancel the dentist on 25 October. We are opening IKEA of the 1980s. With prices from the 1960s. Opening at

Figure 2.10 Ad, 'Learning How to Pronounce,' 1985. (Used with the permission of Inter IKEA Systems B.V. © Inter IKEA Systems B.V.)

9 am on Thursday,' 'Get well by 25 October. We are opening . . .,' 'Don't get married on 25 October. We are opening. . . .'[132]

The advertising for the opening also contained a warning: 'Count on queues, count on a crush. Don't blame us. You have been warned.' Following the opening there were ads devoted to IKEA's new slogan: 'Not For the Rich. But for the Wise' [Inte för de rika. Men för de kloka] and to the new notion of a 'glamorous high street' [Fina gatan] which alluded to exclusive shops in exclusive neighborhoods. The message was self-evident: at IKEA there were cheaply-priced products that were just as good as the more expensive variants in the high street. And not only that, at times the products looked just the same too.

An advertisement for beds echoed the saying: 'As you make your bed so you must lie on it.' The right side of the ad showed a man lying on a bed from IKEA. The price of both mattress and headboard was SEK 860. On the left of the picture another man is seen lying on the floor while the written message points out that the same sum of money spent at an exclusive high-street store would only purchase the headboard and the runners. The slogan on another advertisement reads: 'Did you hear about the man who bought such expensive glasses that he could not afford any brandy?' On one side of the ad are eight handmade brandy glasses for SEK 230, while on the other side there are eight machine-made brandy glasses together with a large bottle of Rémy Martin cognac: 'You get almost the same quality as in an expensive high-street store where you can buy the exclusive product from the famous factory . . . We'll raise our glasses to that' (Figure 2.11).[133]

Figure 2.11 Ad, 'Hörde du om mannen som köpte så dyra glas att han inte hade råd med cognac?' [Did you hear about the man who bought such expensive glasses that he could not afford any brandy?], early 1980s. (Used with the permission of Inter IKEA Systems B.V. © Inter IKEA Systems B.V.)

The message of the advertisement was that people get more for their money at IKEA and that furniture and household utensils looked just the same as wares from expensive competitors. Sometimes the expensive brands were even mentioned by name.[134] In some ads complete rooms are compared. Those from the exclusive high-street shop are empty apart from one or two minor items while the rooms from IKEA are fully furnished. Another ad compares very similar kitchens: 'One kitchen costs SEK 8,469. The other just SEK 4,477. Which do you prefer?'[135]

In this context it is easy to see IKEA as a cheeky imitator, cleverly emphasizing that the name of the game is follow-my-leader. But the advertising and its rhetoric also suggest a real concern for justice. There is an implication that IKEA is doing something positive for people with limited means. The store becomes a sort of Robin Hood, taking from the rich (copying exclusive high-street stores) and giving to the poor (the mass of people).

IKEA has often been accused of stealing other people's designs.[136] One of the authors of *Svenska möbler 1890–1990* (1991) writes: 'With regard to IKEA's designs people in the industry claim that the company sows and reaps where it has not ploughed or harrowed. There are numerous copies and they have sold well.'[137] Others have leapt to IKEA's defense and rejected the accusations with the claim that designers, architects and artists have always been inspired by earlier designs, which means that the boundaries are flexible.[138] Some people counter the criticism by nonchalantly referring to Jean Baudrillard's postmodernist argument that it is no longer possible to erect boundaries between original and copy, or between true and false.[139]

There is constant discussion of the precise location of the boundaries between inspiration, refinement and copying. Whether or not IKEA plagiarizes more than other manufacturers is an interesting question but it is not the principal focus of this book. The fact that the table called 'Lövet,' which was the product that led to the introduction of flat packaging at IKEA, has gained a special place in the company's historiography may seem ironic, given that the product can be regarded as a copy. The table bears striking similarities to the Finnish architect Tapio Wirkkala's 'Leaf' platter (1951) which is, in turn, emblematic of Scandinavian design.[140]

During the 1980s people's attitudes to IKEA changed in Sweden. The brand was no longer associated merely with cheap prices but was also seen as a cheeky innovator with a sense of humor. But the company realized that there was still a large and wealthy group of potential customers who associated IKEA with poor quality. One important step in an attempt to wash off the bargain-price stamp was a campaign entitle 'From Hut to Palace' [Från koja till slott]. In the space of a few years some fifty advertisements were produced showing IKEA's products in exclusive settings and homes. The ads also appeared in financial publications and classy design magazines.[141]

These advertisements were very similar to editorial accounts of people's homes with some of the furniture replaced by products from IKEA. In the settings, the company's own furniture was mixed with design classics, heirlooms and valuable works of art.[142] One advertisement included the Dutch architect Gerrit Rietveld's iconic armchair 'Red and Blue' (1917), while there was a work by Andy Warhol on the wall. Many of the other furnishings were from IKEA. In another advertisement, which might seem to feature a loft in Manhattan, the heading is 'New York? Älmhult?' (Plate 4) while a third ad asks: 'Milano?

Älmhult?' the message of the campaign is basically the same as in earlier advertisements: that IKEA has household products that are just as good as those of exclusive competitors, but at lower prices. Accordingly, the advertisements do not present the products as cheaper copies. The spirit of the ads is, rather, that IKEA is leading the way for some sort of democratization of luxury, giving the common man the opportunity to have just as snazzy a home as a rich person.

During the 1980s there was a stress on the importance of building a durable and resilient corporate identity. IKEA was, in other words, in step with the times, but it was hardly alone in this. Nevertheless, the IKEA brand can be regarded as a forerunner in the field, representing a company that, more than most, succeeded in creating a strong corporate culture with the help of narratives about the origins of the brand, its history and its founder. Originally the central function of storytelling seems not to have been the result of a conscious strategy as expressed in manuals. Rather, the management seems gradually to have realized how well the narratives functioned and, thereafter, seems to have preserved and developed them strategically. Which is not to say that there is always a conscious awareness or insight into the fact that a company is permeated by a narrative culture.[143]

Notes

1 *The Future is Filled With Opportunities*, 2008, p. 6 (IHA).

2 According to IKEA the testament dates from 1976. Just as with *The Future is Filled with Opportunities* the testament has been through several editions and has been translated into several languages. The testament is also included in many different manuals. In this book I have used the 2011 edition: *The IKEA Concept, The Testament of a Furniture Dealer, A Little IKEA Dictionary* (Inter IKEA Systems B.V.: 2011) [1976–2011] (IHA).

3 *IKEA Concept Description* (Inter IKEA Systems B.V., 2000).

4 *IKEA Tillsammans* (Inter IKEA Systems B.V.: 2011) (IHA).

5 The Stone Wall—A Symbol of the IKEA Culture (Inter IKEA Systems B.V., 2012) (IHA). The stone wall has been used as a symbol since the early 1980s. This is not evident from the brochure describing the stone wall and what it stands for, drawing parallels with IKEA. Thus the stone wall serves as a sort of metaphor for the company. It is claimed that the stone wall is 'built to last forever,' and it is compared with the claim that 'Ingvar Kamprad has built IKEA corporate structure to last for ever.' Unpaginated brochure.

6 *Democratic Design. The Story About the Three Dimensional World of IKEA—Form, Function and Low Prices* (Inter IKEA Systems B.V., 1996). Unpaginated catalog (IHA).

7 'Fika' is a Swedish verb and noun that roughly means 'to drink coffee/tea/squash' usually accompanied by something sweet. At the center is an interactive display Explore aimed at staff and IKEA Through the Ages, which is open to the public. *IKEA Tillsammans* (Inter IKEA Systems B.V., 2011) (IHA); Taking part in the course The IKEA Brand Programme 2012.

8 There are about fifty activities to choose from. *IKEA Tillsammans* (2011) (IHA).

9 Interview with Per Hahn, Senior Manager IKEA Culture and Values, June 26, 2012. The testament is regarded as holy writ even by others. See, for example, Torekull 2008, p. 138; *The IKEA Concept* 2011, p. 22 (IHA). The vision 'To create a better everyday life for the many people' is repeated like a mantra in IKEA's internal manuals.

10 *The IKEA Concept* 2011, p. 28 (IHA).

11 *The IKEA Concept* 2011, p. 26.

12 *The IKEA Concept* 2011, p. 27.

13 *The IKEA Concept* 2011, p. 28.

14 *The IKEA Concept* 2011, p. 29.

15 *The IKEA Concept* 2011, p. 31.

16 *The IKEA Concept* 2011, p. 32.

17 *The IKEA Concept* 2011, p. 32.

18 *The IKEA Concept* 2011, p. 37.

19 Björk 1998, pp. 47, 60–1.

20 Torekull 2008, pp. 138, 151, 156.

21 *The IKEA Concept* 2011, p. 6 (IHA).

22 *The IKEA Concept* 2011, pp. 39–58.

23 *The IKEA Concept* 2011, p. 51.

24 The course was created by Mats Agmén. Interview with Mats Agmén, Managing IKEA Concept Monitoring, Inter IKEA Systems B.V., Helsingborg, September 21, 2012. See also the interview with Agmén about the course in the film *IKEAs rötter. Ingvar Kamprad berättar om tiden 1926–1986* (Inter IKEA Systems B.V.: 2007) (IHA).

25 *The Future is Filled With Opportunities* 2008 (IHA).

26 Salzer also confirms this. During her field study she heard the story related by the staff in versions of varying length. See, especially, the chapter 'The Saga About IKEA,' in Salzer 1994, pp. 57–69.

27 *The Future is Filled With Opportunities* 2008, p. 40 (IHA).

28 *The Future is Filled with Opportunities* 2008, p. 65.

29 *The Future is Filled with Opportunities* 2008, p. 73.

30 *The Future is Filled with Opportunities* 2008, p. 79.

31 Salzer 1994, p. 16.

32 Aristotle wrote his Poetics in the fourth century BCE. It explains how a narrative should be constructed for the best effect. He divided a story into a beginning, a middle and an end. For a more detailed description of the parts in relation to corporate storytelling see Klaus Fog, Christian Budtz, Philip Munch and Baris Yakaboylu, *Storytelling. Branding in Practice* (Berlin: Springer, 2010) [2003], pp. 32–46.

33 Kamprad interviewed in Lena Katarina Swanberg, 'Ingvar Kamprad. Patriarken som älskar att kramas,' *Family Magazine*, Nr. 2 (1998), p. 20. There is a very similar claim in another interview in which Kamprad refers to Swedish social democracy and welfare, Staffan Bengtsson, *IKEA The Book. Designers, Products and Other Stuff* (Stockholm: Arvinius, 2010), p. 232.

34 Fog *et al.* 2010, p. 34.

35 http://nikeinc.com/pages/history-heritage (accessed October 8, 2013). For history see also Fog *et al.* 2010, pp. 55–6, 63, 82.

36 Steven Van Belleghen, *The Conversation Company. Boost Your Business Through Culture, People & Social Media* (London: Kogan Page, 2012), p. 69.

37 For Apple's story see Fog *et al.* 2010, pp. 168–9.

38 Under the heading 'Mission Statement' http://www.benjerry/activism and http://www.benjerry.se/vara-varderingar (accessed June 5, 2013).

39 http://www.benjerry.com/flavors/our-flavors/ (accessed June 5, 2013).

40 Joseph Heath and Andrew Potter, *The Rebel Sell: How the Counterculture Became Consumer Culture* (Chichester: Capstone, 2005).

41 Salzer 1994, p. 63.

42 Picture postcard from Inter IKEA Culture Center AB, Älmhult (IHA). There are some forty cards all on the same lines: a challenge or problem is stated together with the IKEA solution to it.

43 For IKEA's dress code see Torekull 2008, p. 163; Salzer 1994, p. 125; Stenebo 2009, p. 126.

44 Salzer 1994, pp. 144–56.

45 IKEA Toolbox (intranet), Helsingborg, December 3, 2010.

46 Salzer (1994) compares corporate culture in Canada and France. Knowledge transfer in the Russian, Chinese and Japanese corporate cultures was studied by Jonsson (2007). There is also a study of how a so-called Swedish management model works in a global context with the focus on IKEA in China. Anders Wigerfeldt, *Mångfald och svenskhet: en paradox inom IKEA* (Malmö: Malmö Institute for Studies of Migration, Diversity and Welfare, Malmö University, 2012).

47 Interview with Hahn, 2012. In due course a settlement was agreed and when STøR ran into financial difficulties the chain was purchased by IKEA in 1992. See Björk 1998, p. 262; Bengtsson 2010, pp. 66–7.

48 *IKEA Concept Description* 2000, pp. 7, 13 (IHA).

49 Information from Hugo Sahlin, June 26, 2013 (IHA).

50 This is described in a succession of manuals. See, for example, *IKEA Concept Description*, 2000; *The IKEA Concept* 2011 (IHA).

51 Atle Bjarnestam 2009, p. 199; Björk 1998, p. 158.

52 *IKEA symbolerna. Att leda med exempel*, Inter IKEA Systems B.V., 2001, p. 28.

53 Salzer 1994, pp. 86–7.

54 Björk 1998, p. 158.

55 *IKEA Match* 1, August 31, 1979 (IHA). There were twelve groups in the project which considered various aspects of the company, including internal information and product supply. Björk 1998, p. 158.

56 Collection of *IKEA Match* (IHA).

57 Bjork 1998.

58 Other internal campaigns: 'Kulturåret,' 'Sparåret' (1990), 'Nytt läge' (1994). Björk 1998, pp. 159–60.

59 Interview with Hahn 2012; *Our Way. The Brand Values Behind the IKEA Concept* (Inter IKEA Systems B.V., 2008) [1999] (IHA).

60 *IKEA Concept Description* 2000, p. 7 (IHA).

61 *The Origins of the IKEA Culture and Values*, Inter IKEA Systems B.V., 2012, p. 25 (IHA).

62 Interview with Hahn 2012; *IKEA Concept Description* 2000. See also *IKEA Values. An essence of the IKEA Concept* (Inter IKEA Systems B.V., 2007) (IHA).

63 *IKEA Concept Description* 2000 (IHA).

64 http://www.IKEA.com/ms/sv_SE/about_IKEA/the_IKEA_way/faq/ (accessed June 13, 2013).

65 Sanna Björling, 'IKEA—Alla tiders katalog,' *Dagens Nyheter*, August 10, 2010.

66 Helene von Reis, IKEA Communications, quoted in Björling 2010.

67 *IKEA Concept Description* 2000, p. 47 (IHA); Salzer (1994) also notes how staff refer to the store in terms of a 'sales machine,' pp. 98, 102–4.

68 The second edition of *Our Way* has the same basic structure as the first but has been modernized graphically; *Our Way. The Brand Values Behind the IKEA Concept* (Inter IKEA Systems B.V., 1999, 2008) (IHA).

69 *Our Way. The Brand Values Behind the IKEA Con*cept, 2008 (IHA).

70 *Our Way Forward. The Brand Values Behind the IKEA Concept* (Inter IKEA Systems B.V., 2011) (IHA).

71 Taking part in internal course The IKEA Programme 2012. Interview with Ola Lindell, Senior Manager Marketing, Stockholm, November 9, 2011. Email from Ola Lindell September 11, 2013.

72 Torekull 2008, p. 160; Atle Bjarnestam 2009, p. 197.

73 Ingvar Kamprad, Framtidens IKEA-varuhus dated October 10, 1989. Document given to the author by a former IKEA employee.

74 Range Presentation (Inter IKEA Systems B.V., 2002) (NLC).

75 Kamprad 1989.

76 Range Presentation (Inter IKEA Systems B.V., 2000, 2001) (NLC).

77 Range Presentation, 2002 (NLC).

78 Range Presentation, 2000, 2001 (NLC).

79 *IKEA Symbolerna. Att leda med exempel* 2001, p. 13 (IHA).

80 Range Presentation, 2002 (NLC); Salzer describes the commercial aspect from 'within,' i.e. how the company encourages increased sales by means of competing with sales volume (Salzer 1994, pp. 96–9).

81 See, for example, Torekull 2008; Lewis 2008, pp. 35; Atle Bjarnestam 2009, pp. 14–15; Swanberg 1998; Björk 1998, p. 42; Stenebo 2009, pp. 43–4. Collected quotes from Kamprad can be found ini Bertil Torekull (foreword), Kamprads lilla gulblå. De bästa citaten från ett 85-årigt entreprenörskap (Stockholm: Ekerlid, 2011).

82 Salzer 1994; Miriam Salzer-Mörling, 'Storytelling och varumärken' in Lars Christensen and Peter Kempinsky (eds), *Att mobilisera för regional tillväxt* (Lund: Studentlitteratur, 2004).

83 Since 1997 the survey has been in the hands of MedieAkademin, Gothenburg. It measures confidence in public institutions, companies and the media. Sören Holmberg and Lennart Weibull from Gothenburg University are responsible for collecting and analyzing the data.

84 Torekull 2008, p. 312.

85 Kamprad quoted in Torekull 2011, p. 26.

86 Torekull 2011, p. 27.

87 Kamprad quoted in *Dagens Industri*, December 17, 1981.

88 The story is recounted in Matts Heijbel, *Storytelling befolkar varumärket* (Stockholm: Blue Publishing, 2010), p. 99.

89 *IKEA Stories 1* (Inter IKEA Systems B.V., 2005), p. 17 (IHA).

90 Torekull 2011, p. 77.

91 Torekull 2011, pp. 89, 90.

92 Torekull 2011, p. 51; Salzer 1994, pp. 132–43.

93 *The IKEA Concept*, 2011, p. 50 (IHA).

94 *The IKEA Concept* 2011, p. 34.

95 Kamprad quoted in Torekull 2011, p. 36.

96 Torekull 2011, pp. 209–10.

97 Kamprad quoted in Torekull 2008, p. 209. Wigforss was one of the Swedish social democrats' leading ideologists and he played a central role in designing welfare policy in his capacity of Finance Minister. He was also critical of the market economy as such.

98 Kamprad quoted in Bengtsson 2010, p. 232.

99 Bengtsson 2010, p. 192.

100 Geoffrey Jones, *Beauty Imagined. A History of the Global Beauty Industry* (Oxford: Oxford University Press, 2010), pp. 163–4.

101 Sjöberg 1998, p. 220 and photographs, unpaginated.

102 Salzer 1994.

103 *IKEA Toolbox* (intranet), June 26, 2013.

104 *IKEA Stories 1*, 2005; *IKEA Stories 3* (Inter IKEA Systems B.V., 2006), *IKEA Stories 1* [DVD] (Inter IKEA Systems B.V., 2005, 2008); *10 Years of Stories From IKEA People* (Inter IKEA Systems B.V., 2008) (IHA).

105 *10 Years of Stories From IKEA People*, 2008, p. 26 (IHA).

106 *IKEA Stories 1*, 2005, p. 7 (IHA).

107 Eron Witzel, Belgium, *IKEA Stories 1*, 2005, pp. 7–8 (IHA).

108 Laurie Hung, Canada, *IKEA Stories 1*, 2005, p. 23 (IHA).

109 Gerwin Reinders, the Netherlands, *IKEA Stories 1*, 2005, p. 32 (IHA).

110 http://www.IKEA.com/ms/en_GB/about_IKEA/the_IKEA_way/history/1940_1950.html (accessed June 13, 2013). Se även *IKEA Stories 1*, 2005, p. 30.

111 Roland Norberg, Sweden, *IKEA Stories 1*, 2005, p. 24 (IHA).

112 *BILLY—30 år med BILLY* (IMP Books AB for IKEA FAMILY, 2009).

113 *BILLY—30 år med BILLY* 2009, p. 41.

114 *BILLY—30 år med BILLY* 2009, p. 53.

115 The story is recounted in Linda Rampell, *Designdarwinismen#ot* (Stockholm: Gábor Palotai Publisher, 2007), p. 95.

116 The story appears on the company's website under the heading 'Heritage.' http://www.cremedelamer.com/heritage (accessed June 22, 2013).

117 Dwayne D. Gremler, Kevin P. Gwinner and Stephen W. Brown (2001), 'Generating Positive Word-of-Mouth Communication Through Customer-Employee Relationships,' *International Journal of Service Industry Management*, 12/1 (2001), pp. 44–59.

118 The stories can be found on the company's website divided into a number of categories. http://www.coca-colacompany.com/stories/coca-cola-stories (accessed June 1, 2013).

119 *Svenska folkets möbelminnen* (Inter IKEA Systems B.V., 2008).

120 The Brindfors advertising agency also worked with other agencies outside Sweden with the aim, for example, of explaining what IKEA stands for. Interview with Hans Brindfors, 20 January 2012; interview with Ola Lindell 2011. Lindell worked at Brindfors in the 1980s and later joined IKEA.

121 Marketing Communication. *The IKEA Way* (Inter IKEA Systems B.V., 2010) (IHA).

122 Interview with Lismari Markgren 2011.

123 Just about everyone interviewed in this book emphasizes the importance of Brindfors. On collaboration between IKEA and Brindfors see also Lars A. Boisen, *Reklam. Den goda kraften* (Stockholm: Ekerlids förlag, 2003), pp. 120–33.

124 On the creative revolution see Andrew Cracknell, *The Real Mad Men. The Remarkable True Story of Madison Avenue's Golden Age, When a Handful of Renegades Changed Advertising for Ever* (London: Quercus, 2011).

125 Graphic design was by Helmut Krone. See Cracknell 2011, pp. 83–100.

126 Cracknell 2011, pp. 83–100.

127 Brindfors was neither the first nor the only Swedish advertising agency to be influenced by the creative revolution. One early and prominent example is Stig Arbman AB whose advertising from the 1950s was strongly influenced by the American pioneers. Boisen, 2003, pp. 25–6.

128 Rand produced the riddle in a poster for IBM in 1981. See Steven Heller, *Paul Rand* (London: Phaidon, 2007), p. 157.

129 The advertisement was created by the American Deutsch agency as part of a campaign to position IKEA and to distinguish the brand from others on the American market. Work on the campaign was preceded by a week of courses at the Brindfors agency in Stockholm. Email from Ola Lindell, August 20, 2012.

130 Boisen 2003, p. 120.

131 Interview with Brindfors 2012; Boisen 2003.

132 Interview with Brindfors 2012. Advertisements/copies from Hans Brindfors' private collection owned by the author. The advertisements are from the early 1980s but exact dates are not given. Many of Brindfors' advertisements can be found in the archive at Landskrona Museum.

133 Advertisements/copies from Hans Brindfors' private collection owned by the author.

134 An advertisement for beds compares IKEA's beds with products from the Swedish company Dux.

135 Advertisements/copies from Hans Brindfors' private collection owned by the author.

136 There were both sweeping accusations and specific court cases. Both the Swedish company Baby-Björn and the America Maglite company sued IKEA. Atle Bjarnestam 2009, p. 215.

137 Monica Boman, 'Den kluvna marknaden' in Monica Boman (ed.), *Svenska möbler 1890–1990* (Lund: Signum, 1991), p. 427.

138 Atle Bjarnestam 2009, pp. 215–17.

139 Bengtsson 2010, pp. 64–5.

140 IKEA was not responsible for the design of the table which was purchased from a supplier. Information from Hugo Sahlin, IKEA Historical Archives, June 26, 2013. Wirkkalla's dish was selected as 'The Most Beautiful Product of 1951' by the American magazine House Beautiful and is regarded as an icon of Scandinavian design. For example, both the poster for the Design in Scandinavia exhibition, and the catalog cover were based on the dish. Widar Halén and Kerstin Wickman (eds), *Scandinavian Design Beyond the Myth. Fifty Years of Design From the Nordic Countries* (Stockholm: Arvinius, 2003), p. 59.

141 Interview with Lennart Ekmark December 16, 2011. Ekmark had a succession of leading positions in IKEA from the 1960s to the 1990s. See interview with Ekmark in Bengtsson 2010, pp. 149–57 and in Bengtsson (ed.), *IKEA at Liljevalchs* (Stockholm: Liljevalchs konsthall, 2009). Unpaginated catalog; Olle Anderby, 'Intervju med Lennart Ekmark. Om reklam i allmänhet—om IKEA:s i synnerhet,' *Den svenska marknaden*, 4/5 (1983), pp. 20–3; Uuve Snidare, 'Han möblerar världens rum,' VI, 32/33 (1993), pp. 12–15.

142 Interview with Ulla Christiansson, Stockholm, December 22, 2011. The interior designs shown in the advertisements were produced by Christiansson and Love Arbén.

143 Interview with Helen Duphorn, Head of Corporate Communication, IKEA Group and Lena Simonsson-Berge, Global Communication Manager, IKEA Retail Services, Helsingborg, June 25, 2013.

3
SWEDISH STORIES AND DESIGN

IKEA's Swedish profile was not part of the original concept. Until 1961 the name of the company was spelt in the French manner with an accent on the 'e': Ikéa (Figure 3.1).[1] Names of products stimulated associations to Italy, France and the USA: 'Antoinette,' 'Lido,' 'Capri,' 'Milano,' 'Piccolo' and 'Texas.'[2] The Swedish profile did not develop until the company began to expand abroad.

True, in the 1970s one finds a number of national markers such as moose and Vikings in Germany, Canada and Australia, IKEA also presented itself as a different and innovative furniture store in what was otherwise a rather conservative industry, while Swedes were seen as slightly cranky, a nation of strange customs and traditions (Plate 5 and Figure 3.2). In Germany the country slogan announced: 'Das unmöglische Möbelhaus aus Schweden' [The Impossible Furniture Store from Sweden], while in France the store claimed: 'Ils Sont Fous ces Suédois' [Swedes Are a Bit Crazy].

Parallel with the introduction of the company's first trademark manual in 1984 the moose and Vikings disappeared.[3] But the national identity was strengthened. 'Swedishness' became the core of the brand's narrative and its corporate culture while the profile became increasingly homogeneous and formalized. A sort of filtered Swedishness was applied to all the company's stores wherever they were in the world. This culture was introduced using concrete markers and aesthetically and linguistically powerful images as well as fairly abstract notions about Sweden and Swedishness.

In 1981 the soul of the brand was launched in a legendary and award-winning advertisement with the smart heading: 'The Soul of IKEA' (Plate 6).[4] A photograph shows a verdant landscape. The sky is blue and a long dry-stone wall runs through the endless countryside. There are no products or price tickets. The point of the image is to communicate the company's roots in the rural Swedish province of Småland. In small letters beneath the photograph there is a text explaining how the stony earth has obliged generations of people from Småland to live frugally and modestly while preserving their independence: 'This is the true soul of IKEA: Giving you a comfortable, tasteful and cheap home. A home that you can afford . . . We achieve this by being obstinate and persevering. By denying the impossible. This is IKEA. The dry-stone walls of Småland run through our hearts.'[5] From this time onwards the dry-stone wall comes to be used increasingly as a symbol of IKEA, an illustration of characteristics such as hardworking and persevering.

The advertisement can be seen as a powerful starting point for making IKEA Swedish, using markers for commercial ends as tools for profiling the brand in a global arena.[6] But

Figure 3.1 Logo, 'Ikéa,' 1948–1949. (Used with the permission of Inter IKEA Systems B.V. © Inter IKEA Systems B.V.)

the aim of this chapter is not to reveal myths about Swedishness, nor to monitor the extent to which IKEA's Swedish profile relates to what is experienced as Swedish in Sweden. Against a background repertoire of conflicting symbols, myths and ideas the aim is, rather, to explore which phenomena they have refined and emphasized and this, in turn, requires a historical context. What are Swedish ideals, norms and values in IKEA's version? How are these communicated and where do they come from? The second part of the chapter analyzes the way in which the product range is used to promote the Swedishness aspect.

IKEA has long worked with something that they call 'Swedishness.'[7] But what is typically Swedish? Does Swedishness really exist and, if it does, what does it consist of? Who is responsible for defining the Swedish national character and is this constant for all Swedes? Sinful Swedish blonds, safe cars, ABBA, Vikings, moose and sorrowful figures from an Ingmar Bergman film are just some of the many different phenomena that are associated with Sweden. There is no direct template that tells us what is Swedish or that points to the peculiarities of the national character.[8]

What we perceive as Swedish is governed by a whole array of ideas, traditions, histories and fictions. The national identity can be understood as a series of narratives of a sense of community which is contrasted with other narratives and other communities. This particular sense of community with others has had great importance in modern theories about the nation as such. Starting from the work of Benedict Anderson, researchers have maintained that the sense of being a nation relies on a feeling of

Figure 3.2 Ad, 'IKEA is Closing.' (Used with the permission of Inter IKEA Systems B.V. © Inter IKEA Systems B.V.)

community.[9] But this is a community of anonymity since the basis of our fellowship is nothing more than precisely the conception of a common nation: we Swedes. But it also involves similarity and one can perhaps describe the community of the nation as a sort of desire for a national we, a we that is shared by all and that thinks in the same way.

Groups and cultures also define themselves by constructing self-images. Traditions, customs and beliefs are adapted and renegotiated in order to fit in with a national framework and the national culture or group is generally regarded as superior to others. Sweden and Swedishness are thus concepts that can be loaded with different meanings depending on the purpose and the frame of reference. A desire to present a homogeneous and attractive national character can be seen in various contexts. For many years, everything from government authorities to commercial brands have been used as national markers with a view to positioning and profiling oneself. An obvious example of this, and almost a caricature, is the car industry in which Swedish safety and reliability compete with Italian elegance and German efficiency.[10]

There are many images of Sweden in circulation and these are often contradictory. At times the country is presented as a miracle of futuristic functionalism while at other times it appears as a highly traditional country, a rural idyll on the outskirts of Europe. Over the centuries Swedish men have been portrayed as hardy pugilists from deep in the forests, but also as rather dull, over-civilized weaklings. Equally paradoxical is the image of Swedish women who are sometimes portrayed as hard-line feminists and sometimes as scantily dressed patsies. At the beginning of the twentieth century Swedes were considered to be brave, valiant, carefree and humane. Half a century later they were talented and good organizers while a few decades after that they had become conflict-avoiding, serious, shy and believers in common sense.[11]

The narratives naturally build on stereotypes. Certain behaviors and characteristics are highlighted while others are ignored. This does not necessarily mean that the national character is purely a product of the imagination.

Blue and yellow linguistics

The logotype is certainly IKEA's most prominent nationalist marker. That it is yellow and blue, that is to say the same colors as the Swedish flag is, of course, no accident. Logotypes are generally regarded as the single most important aspect of a brand's visual identity. Or, as Milton Glaser so appositely puts it: 'The logo is the entry point to the brand.'[12]

Logotypes generally say something about the character of the company. The Jaguar car company's leaping jaguar suggests that the company's cars share the same qualities of speed and elegance as the animal. And Playboy's logo has obvious associations with the magazine's focus on sex. The Playboy rabbit can hardly be confused with his cousin Thumper in Walt Disney's *Bambi*. The bright eyes and the imposing bowtie also suggest style and status. Many logos are characterized by simplification and stylization. The antithesis is the handwritten variety which suggests a guarantee as well as communicating quality and reliability: Cartier, Harrods, Leica and Paul Smith, for example.[13]

Plate 1 'Functional. Not Fancy.' (From *Our Way. The Brand Values Behind the IKEA Concept*. Used with the permission of Inter IKEA Systems B.V. © Inter IKEA Systems B.V.)

Plate 2 Ingvar Kamprad among co-workers, 1999. (Used with the permission of Inter IKEA Systems B.V. © Inter IKEA Systems B.V.)

Plate 3 Ad, 'Embrace Change,' 2009. (Used with the permission of Inter IKEA Systems B.V. © Inter IKEA Systems B.V.)

Plate 4 Ad, 'New York? Älmhult!,' mid-1980s. (Used with the permission of Inter IKEA Systems B.V. © Inter IKEA Systems B.V.)

Plate 5 Ad with Viking. In the 1970s IKEA used national markers such as moose and Vikings in Germany, Canada and Australia. (Used with the permission of Inter IKEA Systems B.V. © Inter IKEA Systems B.V.)

Plate 6 Ad, 'IKEAs själ' [The Soul of IKEA], 1981. (Used with the permission of Inter IKEA Systems B.V. © Inter IKEA Systems B.V.)

Plate 7 IKEA's logotype in red and white. (Used with the permission of Inter IKEA Systems B.V. © Inter IKEA Systems B.V.)

Plate 8 IKEA Food Packaging. (© Stockholm Design Lab, Stockholm.)

Plate 9 Carl Larsson, 'Blomsterfönstret,' Ur 'Ett Hem,' (NMB 268. © Nationalmuseum, Stockholm.)

Plate 10 Interior from 'Stockholm' collection. (Used with the permission of Inter IKEA Systems B.V. © Inter IKEA Systems B.V.)

Plate 11 Bed 'Skattmansö,' from 'IKEA 1700-tal' collection, 1993. (Used with the permission of Inter IKEA Systems B.V. © Inter IKEA Systems B.V.)

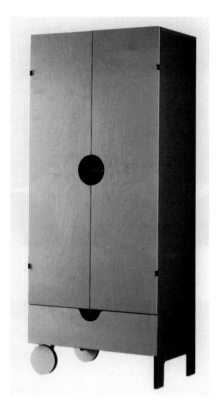

Plate 12 'PS IKEA SKÅP,' Thomas Sandell, 1995. (Used with the permission of Inter IKEA Systems B.V. © Inter IKEA Systems B.V.)

Plate 13 Ad, 'NY Gets Flat Packed.' New York City's first IKEA Store, 2008. (Used with the permission of Inter IKEA Systems B.V. © Inter IKEA Systems B.V.)

Plate 14 Ad, 'Länge leve mångfalden' [Long Live Diversity], 2008. (Used with the permission of Inter IKEA Systems B.V. © Inter IKEA Systems B.V.)

Plate 15 'Swedish.' (From *Our Way. The Brand Values Behind the IKEA Concept.* Used with the permission of Inter IKEA Systems B.V. © Inter IKEA Systems B.V.)

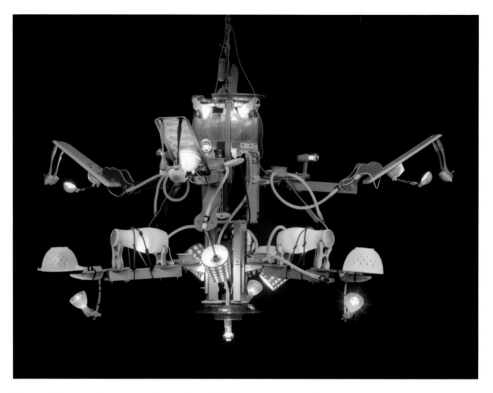

Plate 16 Lamp, Anders Jakobsen, 2005. (© Nationalmuseum, Stockholm.)

Plate 17 Catalog: same product, different country. Part of a page from IKEA's 2013 catalog distributed in the United Kingdom (right) and in Saudi Arabia (left). (Used with the permission of Inter IKEA Systems B.V. © Inter IKEA Systems B.V.)

In the case of IKEA the logo is all about Swedishness. The blue and yellow emblem was introduced in 1984 when it replaced a red and white variant (Plate 7). The stores came to be painted blue with a yellow logo added on the façade. Staff uniforms are color-coded in the same way.[14] The Swedish marker is accompanied by a Nordic-sounding product name which includes the letters å, ä, or ö: the Tylösand sofa is a 'Tylösand' whether the store is in Los Angeles or in Stockholm.[15] The non-Scandinavian names that were used in the past have disappeared.

Products are named in accordance with a special system. Sofas and coffee tables are given Swedish place names while textiles take their names from places in Denmark or use girls' names. Lamps get their names from seas and lakes; beds take their names from places in Norway while carpets generally have Danish names. Chairs often have boys' names or Finnish names while outdoor furniture is named after islands in Scandinavia. Children's products are given adjectives or animal names.[16]

Another concrete national symbol is the food at IKEA. The company does not just sell home furnishings but is also Sweden's largest exporter of processed foods. The store restaurants serve meatballs and there are rusks and preserved herrings on the shelves of the food store. IKEA's first restaurant opened back in 1959 but it was not until 1983 that the emblematic Swedish dish of meatballs with potatoes and cowberries was put on the menu.[17] Minced meat shaped into little balls is served in many other countries but Sweden seems to have monopolized the meatball concept internationally. Meatballs are linked to 'Swedishness' on what Roland Barthes terms a mythical level.[18] And IKEA has, in turn, laid claims to the dish.

Some of the stores serve local specialties. But a large part of the menu is identical throughout the world and this holds true for the in-store food departments which are known as 'Swedish Food Market' and which sell all sorts of Swedish specialties. In 2006 the company launched a series of foodstuffs in which the product names were based on the Swedish name (Plate 8) for the ingredient: 'Dryck Fläder' [Elderflower drink], 'Sill Dill' [Dill-flavored herring] and 'Knäckebröd' [Crispbread]. Major Swedish holidays and traditions are observed in the food stores which feature user-friendly recipes for Swedish dishes and pastries, not least cinnamon buns.[19]

The nature-loving Swedes and the thrifty people of Småland

The country landscape featured in the 'IKEA's soul' advertisement is just one of many idyllic pictures of nature that are used to allude to something specifically Swedish. A passion for nature is, in itself, hardly original. Time and again photographs of wood anemones, glades of delicate birch trees, silent lakes, moss-covered rocks and bountiful fields are used as central markers for pointing to something fundamentally Swedish.[20] The coupling to nature is, however, relatively recent and the Swedish landscape has by no means always been presented as attractive in itself.

In Sweden during the nineteenth century, nature was regarded as hard and rugged, characterless and dull. The ideal, as far as nature was concerned, was the park landscape of southern Europe. It was only with the development of a romantic nationalism that a new conception of Swedish nature was formulated. Now it was seen as altogether fantastic and the Swedes came to regard themselves as lovers of nature. The rhetoric pertaining to the affinity between a people and their type of habitat is hardly unique to Sweden but has been employed in similar fashion in other countries; not least in the UK.[21]

In Sweden, a calm and often melancholy landscape played an important part in the construction of a new Swedish identity and gained almost metaphoric significance.[22] IKEA has adopted and promoted such established romantic-nationalist notions and stereotypes: 'In Sweden, nature plays a vital part in people's lives as well as their homes. In fact, one of the best ways to describe Swedish home-furnishing style is to look at Swedish nature—full of light and fresh air, yet restrained and unpretentious.'[23]

In the spirit of romantic nationalism, the landscape was seen as being different, more attractive and more beautiful than nature in other countries. And nature was also portrayed as somehow democratic with an ability to bridge class barriers: faced with nature, all Swedes are equal, regardless of whether they are poor or rich. In one sense, the Swedish countryside really does belong to the people. There is, in Sweden, a legal right of common entry which guarantees everyone access to the countryside even where the land is privately owned. Right of entry to the countryside is much more restricted in other countries.

The notion of the Swede's passion for her own countryside was formulated by a scientific and cultural elite and gained a footing among increasing numbers of people over the years. The Swedish Tourism Association [STF] was founded as early as 1885, challenging people to enjoy outdoor recreation with the motto: 'Get to know your country!' And generations of schoolchildren have come face to face with the countryside and the animals that live there on obligatory excursions as well as through lyrical descriptions of nature in literature. The cliché about how much Swedes love nature must be seen in a perspective that includes socialization and propaganda.[24]

Just as in other cultures, Swedes associate myths and sayings with particular geographic regions. And in IKEA's allusions to all things Swedish there is an important regional element: the province of Småland. Kamprad's own roots in Småland have been turned into a virtue and the particular characteristics that are ascribed to the province are now part of IKEA's corporate identity: 'The IKEA concept, like its founder, was born in Småland. This is a part of southern Sweden where the soil is thin and poor. The people are famous for working hard, living on slender means and using their heads to make the best possible use of the limited resources they have. This way of doing things is at the heart of the IKEA approach to keeping prices low.'[25]

IKEA's definition of the province of Småland and its people could hardly be more stereotypical than it already is. As with the clichéd references to nature, the roots of this are to be found in the romantic-nationalist movement. Småland originally consisted of a number of smaller districts which were regarded as 'small lands' [små länder] and literature from the sixteenth, seventeenth and eighteenth centuries testifies to a somewhat patronizing view of the region. The inhabitants of Småland were regarded as unreliable and underhand, though with the development of the romantic-nationalist movement a more positive view of the local population grew up and the notion developed that the stony soil was an important attribute of the inhabitants' character. Rather than being classed as stingy they became innovative, frugal and cunning.[26]

The global IKEA narratives internationalize Swedishness and the company's roots in Småland: 'Småland meets the world.'[27] Expansion has meant that high-level managers are not now necessarily Swedes. At IKEA they maintain that 'Swedishness' is not a matter of passports: 'One cannot say that, just because you come from Sweden or from Småland itself that you have more IKEA values, there are numerous non-Swedes who have equally good IKEA values.'[28]

Welfare and the welfare state

But IKEA also creates an essentially Swedish self-image by alluding to modernity, democracy, and social and economic justice just as frequently as using romantic images of the countryside: 'IKEA was founded when Sweden was fast becoming an example of the caring society, where rich and poor alike were well looked after. This is also a theme that fits well with the IKEA vision.'[29]

Portraying Sweden as a model north-European society where unemployment and social distinctions hardly exist has been challenged by people both on the right and on the left. Behind this national façade of normality and harmony there are narratives that testify to a different reality. But, at the same time, the picture of Sweden as a harmonious model country, free from poverty and injustice, has a foundation in the real world.

Between 1920 and 1965 Sweden was transformed from a poor country to a welfare state with a high standard of living. The Social Democrats, who formed the government from the 1930s to the 1970s, introduced a number of reforms, including unemployment insurance, a government-run labor exchange, a legal right to an annual holiday, child allowances, and a national pension scheme. Taken together, these measures ensured a level of social and financial security hardly matched by other countries. People saw the government as being responsible for guaranteeing people a reasonable standard of living even if they were unemployed, ill or old.[30] And so, in Sweden, the notion of welfare is a much broader concept than that expressed by, for example, the British welfare state. While the British welfare state is associated with benefit checks for those who risk falling by the wayside, the Swedish notion of welfare makes it a central aspect of social organization.

One important chapter in this positive view of Sweden was written by Marquis Childs in his book *Sweden. The Middle Way* (1936). The book mapped out a path somewhere in between American capitalism and Soviet socialism.[31] What was later to be termed the 'Swedish model,' Childs characterized as including an expansive corporate sector, nurtured by both the labor unions and the employers who came to their agreements without the government being involved. Also important to this middle way were the Social Democrats' focus on social security and welfare programs.

The notion of the 'folkhem' or Swedish welfare state was commonly used as a synonym for the 'Swedish model.' The 'folkhem' is particularly associated with the leader of the Social Democrats Per Albin Hansson. In a famous speech he made in 1928 he likened the state to a home characterized by equality, concern, cooperation and helpfulness.[32] The 'home' was a metaphor for the nation free from privilege or deprivation. No one should be left outside and the Social Democrats' welfare program included actively seeking to solve the shortage of housing, securing financial benefits for families and improving people's health.

The modernization of Swedish society built on the idea of collective progress, but it can also be regarded as the construction of an identity. It was not just a matter of ensuring material security. The welfare policy also had a more abstract and metaphoric element: the right to belong, which was a form of emotional security. The construction of the Swedish welfare state brought with it a sense of pride and welfare became central to the process of creating a modern identity for Sweden. The social and financial security linked up with the sense of national community and solidarity and was regarded as specifically Swedish.[33]

In sum, it is these ideas about community and solidarity that IKEA makes use of in its definition of the northern country that has discovered the right political mix. A book entitled *Democratic Design*, published by IKEA in 1995, maintains that: 'It [IKEA] grew up in Sweden and its heart remains there to this very day. And, as everyone who has grown up in Sweden has learnt—either from their Dad, or from society in general—people who are not all that well off should be given the same opportunities as people who are. It's hardly surprising that, as a Swedish company, IKEA espouses Swedish values.'[34]

The term 'folkhem' is not just used as a metaphor for the nation. The family home literally became a hub around which the welfare state was constructed and an apartment was regarded as a citizen's right. Enough homes had to be created so that they were available to everyone and people needed to be taught how to furnish their homes in the best possible way. In Sweden there is a long tradition of trying to reform popular taste by teaching people what represents good taste and what does not; right and wrong, wisdom and foolishness.[35]

Beauty for all

The Swedes' interest in the home is a twentieth century phenomenon. In the beginning of the century there was a shortage of housing and many existing apartments could hardly be classed as fit for human habitation. The towns could not house all the people who moved into them from the countryside and large families lived in overcrowded conditions in dark tenements. Poverty was widespread. Domestic hygiene and public health were poor. And there were moral aspects to critics' interest in the home too. Official policy was to provide accommodation for everyone, but there were also demands that apartments should be furnished in a particular fashion. In an influential essay entitled *Beauty in the Home* (1899) Ellen Key forcefully maintained that there was a connection between outer and inner: a person living in beautiful surroundings also became a better and happier person.[36] The author took the view that beauty could change and refine a person and she claimed that everyone had the right to live in such surroundings. Her ideas were characterized by a social and democratic commitment.

One problem that Key noted was that popular taste was underdeveloped. The mass of people simply did not know what was beautiful and, accordingly, needed to be educated in this dimension.[37] Inspired by William Morris and the Arts and Crafts movement, Key linked beauty with simplicity, appropriateness, harmony and honesty, while she also had very concrete rules and suggestions: like buying cheap wallpaper and hanging it with the backside outwards in order to avoid the pattern. Her 'best' advice was that people should avoid distorted and overly complex forms, as well as showy, checkered or garish colors and to choose simple forms and monotone colors instead.[38]

A model dwelling, in this regard, was the home of artists Carl and Karin Larsson's in Sundborn, which provided an aesthetic framework to Key's visions. Carl Larsson portrayed his home in a series of watercolors, published in book form in 1899 (Plate 9). The interiors of the Larsson home represented a radical break with the affluent middle-class home of the nineteenth century with its representative furnishing. Rather than large, heavy, and dark items of furniture, a characteristic of the Larsson home was simplicity, light interiors, bright colors and natural materials. The effect signaled contentment and community. The happy family life and the furnishings seemed to go hand in hand.

Larsson's watercolors featuring his blond, blue-eyed children at home, were reproduced in enormous numbers and, in due course, became the very incarnation of everything Swedish thus providing a stylistic ideal that IKEA could refer to: 'In the late 1800s, the artists Carl and Karin Larsson combined classical influences with warmer Swedish folk styles. They created a model of Swedish home furnishing design that today enjoys worldwide renown.'[39]

Carl Larsson's *A Home* launched a particular aesthetic, but also a lifestyle that came to be regarded as essentially Swedish: an informal, relaxed family life with children at the center. The Larsson home was welcomed by Key who also had ideas about children and education, arguing that children needed leisure and opportunities for developing their imagination and feelings in free play. Rather than controlling, inhibiting and subduing children, adults should adapt to their children's own needs and activities. Many other Swedish educational reformers were subsequently to use similar language.[40]

Key's ideas were further disseminated by Gregor Paulsson, a socially committed art historian who was also strongly influenced by the artists and architects connected with the Deutscher Werkbund. In line with many of the leading thinkers of the German organization, in his book *Better Things for Everyday Life* (1919) Paulsson maintained that if the mass of the population was to have access to beautiful and affordable artifacts then these would have to be manufactured in a rational manner using machines (Figure 3.3). Towards the end of the 1920s Paulsson helped to plan the *Stockholm Exhibition of 1930* in which modernist ideas were launched on a wide front (Figure 3.4).[41] And in his manifesto-like *acceptera* (1931) Paulsson and his co-authors insisted that the solution to the housing shortage and to the appalling conditions in which many people were forced to live was to rationalize the building industry. In the following year the Social Democrats came to power, promising to solve the housing situation; and it is not surprising that they supported the modernist architects who claimed to have the solution.[42]

Beauty in the Home, Better Things for Everyday Life and *acceptera* were of great importance to the dominant agenda and public discourse on architecture and interior

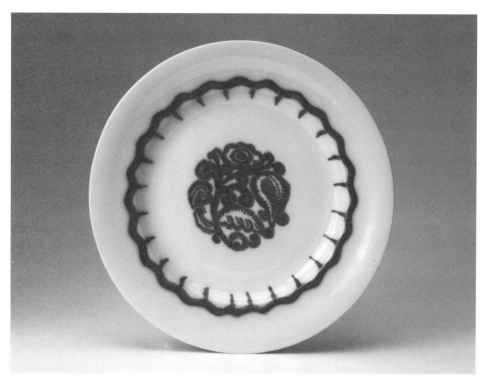

Figure 3.3 Wilhelm Kåge, Soup plate, manufactured by Gustavsberg, Sweden, 1917. Known as the 'Arbetarservisen' [Worker's service] with motif 'Blå lilja' [Blue lily]. The range was a deliberate attempt to produce 'good design,' attractive yet inexpensive. (© Nationalmuseum, Stockholm.)

design in Sweden.[43] Housing became a political issue with political solutions. A common denominator of the texts is the understanding of design and architecture as important tools for the development of society. Another shared feature is that the highly normative texts have a perspective of superiority with elements of paternalism and the authoritarian education of people's taste which had its own repercussions.

A government study from the 1940s monitored how people behaved in their homes: How was the home used? Where did people sleep and eat? And was there space for the children? In spite of living in cramped conditions, people were loath to depart from convention and they still maintained a formal drawing room that was scarcely used while the family were cooped up in the other room. Thus some people were unwilling victims of overcrowding while others chose to live in cramped conditions; a situation that the people writing the report attributed to ignorance.[44] And this was something that the 'experts' wanted to cure. They were convinced that people could learn to make better choices if they were instructed by people in the know.

At the same time there was a veritable flood of courses and exhibitions, as well as columns of advice in magazines aimed at 'irrational' habits. Ungainly interiors with dark and gloomy furnishings were to be thrown out in favor of slim, light and practical variants.[45] The official rhetoric thus embraced a particular style or ideal: clean, simple and fit for purpose, as well as light and airy. Simply put, an ideal that was termed Swedish by IKEA too: 'The Swedish approach to design is also the basis of the IKEA range, which to this day is developed in Sweden. The home furnishings are modern but not trendy, functional

Figure 3.4 Sigurd Lewerentz, Poster 'Stockholm Exhibition,' 1930. (© Nationalmuseum, Stockholm.)

yet attractive, human-centered and child-friendly, and they represent the fresh, healthy Swedish lifestyle through their carefully chosen colors and materials.'[46]

But it was not just the government that sought to educate people. The furniture and interior-design department which existed at the prestigious NK department store in Stockholm between 1947 and 1965 organized several courses on home furnishing and was the first Swedish store to show furniture in realistic settings; something that was to become an IKEA trademark.[47]

Swedish modern and Scandinavian design

The image of Sweden as a golden mean between socialism and capitalism is a useful marketing aid for Swedish design. The 1930s saw the term 'Swedish Modern' minted as a way of describing a softer modernist style: wood instead of steel tubing, organic forms rather than stiff right angles. The style synchronized with the political middle way and the concept is often claimed as an example of the international success of Swedish designers. But as it has been pointed out, the concept is frequently used in practice to describe furniture manufactured in the USA and designed by American designers.[48] In other words, it was the narrative about Sweden and Swedish design that made a style 'Swedish' rather than the design itself or its origin.

From here it is a relatively short step to the concept of 'Scandinavian design,' which was a sort of construction or strategic alliance for the purposes of trade and marketing. The Nordic countries joined forces during the 1950s and launched a joint aesthetic on the American market. In a succession of contexts such as exhibitions, publications and commercial events, Scandinavia was portrayed as a regional and cultural entity characterized by social responsibility and representing a model democracy with a mutual aesthetic. The joint style was elegant and unassertive without decorative excesses, and usually employed natural materials.[49]

The style proved right for the times. In the era of the cold war, Scandinavian modernism was seen in the USA as offering a warm, soft contrast to strict modernism with its German roots. While the latter was described as being authoritarian, cold and highly regulated, Scandinavian design was seen as humanist and democratic: a modern style that was not overly radical and that was social without being socialist.[50]

The most important step in launching Scandinavian design was an exhibition entitled 'Design in Scandinavia' which toured the USA and Canada from 1954 to 1957. Besides record numbers of visitors and huge publicity, the exhibition was a dream scenario for Scandinavian manufacturers. At the same time that critics praised the exhibition, retail stores mounted all sorts of Scandinavian ventures.[51] That Finland, which is not, strictly speaking, physically part of Scandinavia, was included among the exhibitors scarcely upset anyone at all. After the privations of the war it had become important to Finland to emphasize its independence from the Soviet bloc and design exhibitions were an effective way of establishing a position in the American market.[52]

Few people attach any particular importance to individual differences among the countries involved. On the contrary, the emphasis was on their homogeneity. In his book

Scandinavian Design (1961) Ulf Hård af Segerstad maintained that it was a question of: 'Four countries—one aesthetic culture.'[53] That the term 'Scandinavian' acquired a commercial value is also apparent from the exhibition *Formes Scandinaves* (1968) at the Musée des Arts Décoratifs in Paris. In spite of the fact that the exhibition included items from all of the Nordic countries, for marketing purposes the museum wanted to use the term *Scandinave* in the title rather than the more obscure *Nordique* or *Nord*.[54]

House styles and Swedish collections

During the post-war period Swedish design has been absorbed by the term 'Scandinavian design.' True, IKEA has a Swedish profile but one can claim that it has also launched a sort of budget variant on Scandinavian design for the masses and has, like many other businesses, capitalized on the concept.[55] The Swedish tradition of refining taste has also helped in achieving this end.

During the 1970s IKEA began a more systematic study of how people solve various problems connected with the use of their homes. Lennart Ekmark, who had a key position in IKEA for several decades, was an important factor in this, borrowing information from the Swedish Consumer Agency and the municipal home advisory service, for example.[56] He maintained that one needed a realistic understanding of people's habits and needs regarding their homes and so the concept of 'Living Situations' was coined.[57]

In practice the concept came to function as a tool that is still in use. The tool helps to monitor people's practical domestic phases throughout their lives. There is a primary distinction between homes with children and homes without children. These are the major divisions which can then be divided into subdivisions: families with infants or with older children, young single households where the person has recently left the family home, young couples, single households, older and more well established homes (single or couples).[58]

It took some considerable time before IKEA established a fixed range of products. During the 1970s there were obvious distinctions between stores and the product ranges differed. In time each store came to look increasingly like the next one and IKEA began to look like a homogeneous company. The size of the store still determines the extent of the range, but basically one meets the same products and interiors all over the world.[59] All the decisions as to the range of products, the number of articles, prices, transportation and design are taken by the 'IKEA of Sweden' unit in Älmhult where staff mostly consist of buyers, product developers and product designers.[60] The range is naturally not fixed: some products are removed and others are taken up. Besides the common basic range there is also what is known as a 'Free Range' assortment from which individual stores can make their own choices.

According to Kamprad's testament the basic range should be seen as typically IKEA and, outside Scandinavia, as typically Swedish.[61] Design is, to a great extent, determined by price and from that point of view designers have been particularly important. The aim has been to reduce manufacturing costs by, for example, limiting the amount of materials involved through the use of clever solutions and constructions, adapting measurements to the last millimeter or using residues.[62]

An example is provided by the transport pallet measuring 80 x 120 cm with a maximum loaded height of one meter. As many pieces of a product as possible are to be fitted into this space which makes great demands on the designer. In order to avoid having to transport large numbers of empty pallets in the massive chain of logistics, IKEA now uses disposable pallets which can be can be ground down and the material re-used.[63]

Since the 1990s the IKEA range has been based on a special system that comprises almost 10,000 long- and short-lived items. Some 20–25 per cent of the range is changed every year and as a new product is developing an old one is being phased out since the matrix is, in principle, fixed. But there are a number of classics that have continued as part of the range year after year, including Poäng, Billy and Ivar. This is partially a reflection of the fact that furniture generally has a longer life than textiles and lamps, for example.[64]

This systemization of the range, including everything from furniture and household utensils to textiles, can be described in terms of a matrix and is based on a division into a variety of different styles. Categorization of the products, based on different styles and price levels, was first introduced back in the 1980s and, after its gradual implementation, proved to be a useful tool in determining the IKEA range.[65] With the help of this sophisticated system it is possible for IKEA to keep control of a large number of items, but the development of the range is also a matter of aesthetic profile with a sharper focus on Scandinavian modernism.[66]

All of the products are sorted by style and price level: high, medium, low and breath-taking-item. But they are also divided into categories such as bedroom, kitchen and sitting room depending on function. Over the years the styles have had different names and there have been more of them, though the basic structure remains the same: 'Traditional' (which was formerly known as 'Country'), 'International Modernism,' 'Scandinavian Modernism' and 'Young.'[67] Style groups also have subsections with accessories, for example, being available in both light and dark colors. Each year designers are given a number of colors to work with and this means that the range in each style group becomes more homogeneous. There is no equality between style groups. One style group can thus comprise a small number of items while another has many more products.[68]

The aim of the styles and their subdivisions is to cater for different tastes and preferences. But the categories also determine how the products are presented in the stores and the catalog. The interiors consist of products from different style groups but with one of these being dominant in order to create a more homogeneous look.[69] This communicates a sense that everything 'matches': the sofa with the curtains and the lamp with the coffee table. At regular intervals the styles are described in manuals but the boundaries between them are not razor-sharp and descriptions are relatively sweeping. Thus products that are rather different in expression can be fitted into the same group. Linguistically speaking, the style groups testify to a clear emphasis on modernist styles, particularly a Scandinavian modernism.

Over the years IKEA has commissioned internationally famous designers whose work has been presented anonymously in the catalog and the stores.[70] But since the middle of the 1990s designers have been given much greater prominence. Their names can be found on the label listing information about the product and they feature on photographs in the stores and the catalog. To a much greater extent, designers now function as a marketing ploy. This change of mind is probably related to the current trend where designers are credited with as much importance as the products themselves. In line with other brands like H&M, IKEA has featured its collaboration with well-known designers and this has also come to be seen as an aspect of marketing because working with famous designers generates publicity from the media.[71]

Parallel with restricting the range of products through the matrix of styles IKEA has also launched special collections with a clear Swedish identity. These series can be seen as supplementary collections to the rest of the range and, in this sense, they deviate from the standard collections. The special collections are strategic undertakings aimed at strengthening the Swedish identity and this makes them highly illuminating. Internally they are described as 'Scandinavian Collections' and as 'top-of-the-line.'[72] The special collections have also led to the production of special catalogs in which the products are presented in relation to a central theme in Swedish design history. Roughly at the same time as the 'From cabin to palace' campaign noted above, a succession of furniture was launched that was a little more expensive than the rest of the range, intended to appeal to a 'slightly more adult clientele.'[73] The series, to which a range of household utensils was then added, was named 'Stockholm' (Plate 10). The marketing associated with this collection is evocative of the notion of IKEA being a Robin Hood of the furniture industry. The message is that IKEA wants to give the common man the opportunity to have a home that is as beautiful as the homes of a small number of rich people. As well as emphasizing the modest price, there is also a focus on the craft details, the meticulous choice of materials and the superior quality.[74]

The collection was presented in a brochure entitled *Vackrare vardag* [Beautiful Everyday Life] a paraphrase of Paulsson's motto mentioned above. There are strong similarities between the IKEA products and those of such famous Swedish designers as Carl Malmsten and Josef Frank. These 'sources of inspiration' were not named in this context though the brochure did mention that the items had won prizes for the design: 'Everything has been originally designed by IKEA's designers who are recognized for their skill . . . Despite this, the prices are very low in comparison with other such quality furniture.'[75] The term 'original design' somewhat comically testifies to a feeling that not all the company's designs are absolutely original. And at the same time the brochure mentions similar products from elsewhere.

At the beginning of the 1990s, the 'Stockholm' range was joined by a Gustavian collection (Plate 11). The Gustavian style is a Swedish variant of neo-classicism, somewhat simpler in appearance than the French models. The collection came about following collaboration between IKEA and two government bodies, the Nationalmuseum in Stockholm and the Swedish National Heritage Board. The latter had sought financial help from IKEA to save a culturally valuable collection of Gustavian furniture. IKEA provided finance and, in exchange, was allowed to borrow designs from this collection and to receive help from the museum's experts.[76]

The final result was some forty carefully crafted copies largely made with the same techniques that had been used in making the originals. The items, made of solid timber such as birch, alder and pine, were constructed using wooden plugs and glue. Machines were used where this was practicable but all the ornamentation was cut by hand by craftsmen.[77] Since the items were copies of originals they could have been termed 'pastiches.' On the other hand, they were not just based on original designs or even mere imitations but were, rather, careful copies. All of the products were controlled and stamped by the National Heritage Board with its official seal and the project could be seen, at least partially, as a serious cultural manifestation.

The fact that the project was supported by the two government bodies concerned with the nation's heritage was, of course, beneficial, providing credibility and legitimacy while the collection was launched in typical IKEA fashion. The slogan was the 'People's Furniture' and, just as in the past, the narrative was about IKEA giving people in general the opportunity to own a more beautiful home: 'Should not the majority, rather than a small number, be able to enjoy this exquisite combination of beauty and function?'[78]

A few years later IKEA used a rather similar slogan, 'Design for the People!' in connection with launching IKEA's first PS collection at the Milan Furniture Fair in 1995 (Figure 3.5). The budget store made its entry into the exclusive domains of the design world with an aesthetic that was made for the moment.[79] The collection comprised some forty items by nineteen young but established designers who had been selected after taking part in a competition on the theme of 'Democratic design.'[80] The idea behind 'PS' was that the collection should be seen as a postscript to the regular range but, in point of fact, people read it as meaning 'Products of Sweden.'[81] The misinterpretation was perfectly understandable in that the collection had an explicitly Swedish profile.

The catalog contains photographs of lakes with mirror-smooth surfaces and beautiful groves of birch trees, as well as clichéd descriptions of Swedish design which, it is

Figure 3.5 Design Democratico, exhibition in Milan, 1995. (Used with the permission of Inter IKEA Systems B.V. © Inter IKEA Systems B.V.)

claimed, is based on a distinctive feeling for nature. But a sense of social responsibility is classed as just as fundamental. An essay repeats the customary presentation together with a survey of Swedish design history and we are told how a vision of well-designed but cheap products for ordinary people has been turned into a reality: 'Swedish and Scandinavian design have been famous ever since the beginning of the twentieth century. The Swedish model has also become synonymous with good value, functionality and quality together with an ambition to achieve widespread accessibility. IKEA PS is a complement to IKEA's normal range that aims to emphasize this.'[82]

Despite the fact that several designers were involved, the PS collection had a highly cohesive aesthetic with a simple, undecorated style. One review claimed that: 'Most Swedish of all in Milan was IKEA . . . IKEA has now, following many years of claims of plagiarism, answered with the PS collection.'[83]

On account of the collection's obvious references to a modernist aesthetic and ideology, it is not surprising that the PS collection was generally regarded as self-evidently neo-modernistic (Figure 3.6 and Plate 12).[84] But critics have pointed to the fact that the collection could equally well be interpreted as postmodern pastiche with reproduced fragments of a modernist style.[85]

Images on the global arena

Few companies have quite such an obvious Swedish identity as IKEA, though there are common denominators with other brands that have a Swedish profile. Central orientation points are welfare policy and a simple, unadorned style. Among the best-known of these brands is Volvo which, as early as the 1950s, capitalized on the fact that it produced its cars in Sweden as a guarantee of safety and quality: 'Buy Swedish Quality—Buy a Volvo PV444' (1956).[86] Volvo gradually toned down references to Sweden but, as the national identity was updated and sharpened during the 1990s, the Swedish element was brought to the forefront once again.[87]

The fact that parts of the car relied on components manufactured in other countries was not considered relevant in this context. Just like IKEA, Volvo referred to welfare, social concern, safety and quality: 'If you consider Sweden as a caring society, what would be more caring than a Volvo with its safety? A Swedish company couldn't design and build non-safe products knowingly.'[88] Responsible for the renewal of Volvo's product design was a British designer, an indication that the notion of 'Swedish design' does not necessarily need to involve a Swedish designer. The characteristics associated with Swedish design can, in other words, be applied by people who are not actually Swedes, just like a period wallpaper.[89]

At the same time that Volvo was sharpening its profile so, too, was Scandinavian Airlines (SAS) with the intention of signaling the very quintessence of all that is Scandinavian.[90] Everything from business cards to packaging and web design became subject to a consistent, unembellished graphic-design program. A plain new font, 'Scandinavia,' was created for the graphics and there was an image bank with motifs that were thought to express what was typically Scandinavian (Figure 3.7).[91]

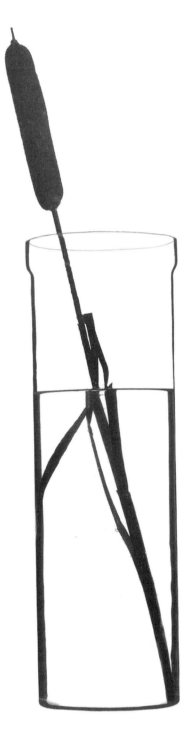

Figure 3.6 'PS IKEA VAS,' Pia Wallén, 1995. (Used with the permission of Inter IKEA Systems B.V. © Inter IKEA Systems B.V.)

Scandinavian

AaBbCcDdEeFfGgHhIiJjKkLlMmNnOoPpQqRrSsTtUu
VvWwXxYyZz1234567890(&.,:?!)§$£ ™

AaBbCcDdEeFfGgHhIiJjKkLlMmNnOoPpQqRrSsTt
UuVvWwXxYyZz1234567890(&.,:?!)§$£ ™

AaBbCcDdEeFfGgHhIiJjKkLlMmNnOoPpQqRrSsTt
UuVvWwXxYyZz1234567890(&.,:?!)§$£ ™

**AaBbCcDdEeFfGgHhIiJjKkLlMmNnOoPpQqRrSs
TtUuVvWwXxYyZz1234567890(&.,:?!)§$£ ™**

SAS98/09/24

Typeface for SAS Scandinavian Airlines by Robin Nicholas, Monotype Typography, Ltd. and Börn Kusoffsky/Kerb Nyberg, Stockholm Design Lab

01

This typeface has been specially created for SAS to act as
the primary SAS typeface for all applications on high-level
communications and all identity implementation. This is the
only sans serif typeface to be used on all SAS applications.

Scandinavian Extra Light	Scandinavian Extra Light Expert	Scandinavian Extra Light CE	Scandinavian Extra Light Cyrillic
Scandinavian Extra Light Italic	Scandinavian Extra Light Italic Expert	Scandinavian Extra Light Italic CE	Scandinavian Extra Light Italic Cyrillic
Scandinavian Light	Scandinavian Light Expert	Scandinavian Light CE	Scandinavian Light Cyrillic
Scandinavian Light Italic	Scandinavian Light Italic Expert	Scandinavian Light Italic CE	Scandinavian Light Italic Cyrillic
Scandinavian Regular	Scandinavian Regular Expert	Scandinavian Regular CE	Scandinavian Regular Cyrillic
Scandinavian Regular Italic	Scandinavian Regular Italic Expert	Scandinavian Regular Italic CE	Scandinavian Regular Italic Cyrillic
Scandinavian Bold	Scandinavian Bold Expert	Scandinavian Bold CE	Scandinavian Bold Cyrillic
Scandinavian Bold Italic	Scandinavian Bold Italic Expert	Scandinavian Bold Italic CE	Scandinavian Bold Italic Cyrillic
Scandinavian Black	Scandinavian Black Expert	Scandinavian Black CE	Scandinavian Black Cyrillic
Scandinavian Black Italic	Scandinavian Black Italic Expert	Scandinavian Black Italic CE	Scandinavian Black Italic Cyrillic

Boeing 737
Boeing 737
Boeing 737
Boeing 737
Boeing 737

ab

Figure 3.7 Font 'Scandinavian.' (Stockholm Design Lab, © Stockholm Design Lab.)

Air travel is a modern form of transportation that can hardly be associated with nature. On the contrary, air travel is the epitome of an ecological threat. But nature came to be used by SAS as a framework and a symbol. Menus and baggage tags were decorated with photographs portraying nature accompanied by such pretentious claims as: 'Luggage is like a poem. It's what's inside that counts.'[92] Just looking Scandinavian was not enough. Flight attendants were trained to behave in a 'Scandinavian' way which, according to SAS, involved being straightforward, simple and unaffected. The familiar form of 'you' was to be used rather than formal modes of address and staff were to be service-minded in a pleasant but not subservient manner.[93]

Absolut Vodka is yet another example of a brand that has emphasized its Swedish origins and is generally regarded as a particularly successful brand-building story. The product was launched in 1979 and its success was hardly due to the contents of the bottle, which is basically alcohol and water. It was the bottle itself that played such an important role. The design of the container is very different from other vodka bottles, being based on old medicine bottles; a simple form in uncolored glass that corresponds to the current image of Swedish design.[94]

Each bottle bears the device 'Country of Sweden' and a text explaining that the vodka is distilled using wheat grown in southern Sweden. The national references are clearly indicated but it is surely not these that have led to the product's success. Rather, it is the spectacular advertising campaigns, associating the product with glamour, exclusivity and eccentricity, featuring fashion, design and art as the context.

From copycat to master of style

As early as his publication *The Testament of a Furniture Dealer*, Kamprad insisted that the product range should reflect IKEA's identity and should send out Swedish signals. In the 1970s the product range was characterized by pine furniture as well as a youthful and unconventional touch.[95] But it was not until later, with the division into specific styles and with profiled collections, that the IKEA range became more of a national identity with regular references to a socially committed Swedish history of design.

An illuminating example of this is the catalog entitled *Design for the People* (1999), in which there was a focus on specific parts of the range, notably the three 'Scandinavian Collections' already mentioned. The tone is very different from that of the 1980s when the marketing hardly concealed the fact that IKEA had products that were very similar to more expensive products elsewhere. Now IKEA is happy to bathe in historic glory. Rather than showing a similar, exclusive piece of furniture, IKEA's products are presented together with descriptions of stylistic ideals, a manifestation that has gained public notice, a publication or the name of a well-known designer.

The products are no longer portrayed as cheap imitations but, rather, as successors. In educative fashion, presentations point to the ideas and aesthetic ideals of the twentieth century which the company claims to have interpreted and realized. In this way IKEA links itself up with positively charged visions of society, integrating them into the corporate culture: 'The quest for beautiful everyday products went on. Later it would be taken up by IKEA.'[96]

At the same time, one may ask how 'Swedish' the range actually is on a design level. 'Billy,' it is claimed, is the world's best-selling bookcase and so one might speculate as to whether the world is becoming 'Swedified' in expression. Or is it a matter of a species of characterless, globalized aesthetic and regimentation? The low prices require large quantities. And the products need to function in Cracow, Paris and Riyadh as well as in Los Angeles. Since IKEA stores throughout the world are intended to have the same range of products, this naturally leads to aesthetic limitations (Plate 13).

Illustrative of this are the company's posters and other visual images. During the 1970s and 1980s the company sold reproductions of well-known works of art by artists like Piet Mondrian and these were also hung inside the stores.[97] Over the years, these posters have been succeeded by other types of images and reproduction rights are purchased from the large picture agencies. Selection and purchasing are governed and motivated by the need to ensure that the images are compatible with IKEA's picture frames and that they harmonize with the rest of the range as well as functioning globally. Sexual, religious or political provocations are, therefore, unthinkable and the end result is, accordingly, rather watered down; a sort of bland embellishment or artistic elevator art. IKEA itself maintains that customers should be able to express their identities through the products.[98] If that is the case, then the identity will surely be rather lacking in expressivity.

The brand defines what is typically Swedish using classical markers which, in an international perspective, stands for something exotic: country settings, green nature, red cottages with white trimmings, as well as welfare programs with social and economic equality. These are well integrated and positively charged images that IKEA uses consciously and that it seeks to associate with the brand while, at the same time, adapting it to commercial usage. But in the narratives, new and more modern forms of Swedishness can be discerned.

During the twenty-first century IKEA has referred both internally and externally to diversity, as is apparent in the campaign 'Long Live Diversity' as well as in the internal project 'The Diversity Plan' (Plate 14).[99] IKEA is no stranger to gay adverts and has run several campaigns featuring gay couples. An IKEA brochure emphasizes that many Swedes have foreign roots and that the company welcomes everyone regardless of their sexuality. This message is illustrated by a photo of a wedding cake decorated with pink icing and showing two men embracing.

One heading claims that 'We Believe In Different Things (Or In Nothing At All)' and this has to do with migration having led to many different faiths being represented in Sweden. The attitude to diversity and disparity is illustrated by a mosaic of photographs of people of different sexes, ages, skin colors, and hair color; and IKEA maintains that the stores can meet everyone's needs and dreams since there are 9,537 products to choose between.[100]

Notes

1 Information from Hugo Sahlin, June, 26 2013 (IHA).

2 *IKEA Catalog*, 1955 (IHA).

3 Information from Hugo Sahlin, June 26, 2013 (IHA).

4 The advertisement was awarded the Swedish advertising prize, 'Guldägget' and many people have noted its importance. See Salzer 1994, pp. 2–3; Atle Bjarnestam 2009, p. 104; Boisen 2003, p.126.

5 The advertisement is in the archive at Landskrona Museum.

6 IKEA often emphasizes that Swedishness is frequently used for profiling the company. See, for example, *Marketing Communication. The IKEA Way* 2010, p. 46 (IHA).

7 Interview with Lismari Markgren 2011.

8 There are numerous studies of Swedish mentality, most of them in Swedish. For a survey in English see, for example, Tom O'Dell, 'Junctures of Swedishness. Reconsidering representations of the National,' *Ethnologia Scandinavica*, 28 (Lund: Folklivsarkivet, 1998), pp. 20–37; Jonas Frykman, 'Swedish Mentality. Between Modernity and Cultural Nationalism' in Kurt Almqvist and Kay Glans, *The Swedish Success Story* (Stockholm: Axel and Margaret Ax:son Johnson Foundation, 2004), pp. 121–32.

9 Anderson 1983, p. 15. Research into notions about national identities is extensive. For a broad survey see Gerard Delanty and Krishan Kumar (eds), *The SAGE Handbook of Nations and Nationalism* (London: SAGE, 2006). For a survey of studies focusing on Sweden see Urban Lundberg and Mattias Tydén (eds), *Sverigebilder. Det nationellas betydelser i politik och vardag* (Stockholm: Institutet för Framtidsstudier, 2008). Other examples are Patrik Hall, *The Social Construction of Nationalism. Sweden as an Example*, Diss. (Lund: University Press, 1998); Kurt Almqvist and Alexander Linklater (eds), *Images of Sweden* (Stockholm: Axel and Margaret Ax:son Johnson Foundation, 2011).

10 The car industry as an example is used in Penny Sparke's *An Introduction to Design and Culture. 1900 to the Present* (London: Routledge, 2004), p. 206.

11 Åke Daun, *Svensk mentalitet. Ett jämförande perspektiv* (Stockholm: Rabén & Sjögren, 1989), p. 223; Jan C.H. Karlsson: 'Finns svenskheten? En granskning av teorier om svenskt folklynne, svensk folkkaraktär och svensk mentalitet' i *Sociologisk Forskning*, Nr. 1, 1994, pp. 41–57.

12 Glaser's dictum appears frequently and in a variety of contexts. See for example http://www. how-to-branding.com/Logo-Design-Theory.htlm (accessed November 25, 2013).

13 For a collection of 1,300 more or less familiar symbols and logotypes together with comments and categorization see Angus Hyland & Steven Bateman, *Symbol* (London: Laurence King Publishing, 2011).

14 The red and white logotype was used in Scandinavia until 1997. Information from Hugo Sahlin, June 26, 2013 (IHA).

15 The basic principle is that names should have a Scandinavian connection, a principle that has become all the more important as IKEA has established itself on the global market. Atle Bjarnestam 2009, p. 209.

16 Atle Bjarnestam 2009, p. 209. The assignment of names is also illustrated in the display *IKEA Explore*, at Inter IKEA Culture Center, Älmhult.

17 Ylva Magnusson, IKEA, interviewed in Thomas Pettersson, 'Så spred IKEA den svenska köttbullen över världen,' *Expressen*, February 21, 2011. It has also been claimed that meatballs were introduced into IKEA back in 1970, see Björk 1998, p. 40.

18 Jonathan Metzger, *I köttbullslandet: konstruktionen av svenskt och utländskt på det kulinariska fältet*, Diss. (Stockholm: Acta Universitatis Stockholmiensis, 2005), p. 30. By 'myth' Barthes means a layer of meaning that is attached to concepts and phenomena which do not actually need to belong there. A possible but not self-evident coupling or a message that parasitizes on a different word or phenomenon. Roland Barthes, *Mythologies* (New York: Hill and Wang, 2012) [1957], pp. 215–74.

19 Almost all of the products are sold under the brand name IKEA Food Service which is a giant in the Swedish food market. In 2010 the brand had a turnover of #eu1.1 billion. Pettersson 2011.

20 Billy Ehn, Jonas Frykman and Orvar Löfgren: *Försvenskningen av Sverige. Det nationellas förvandlingar*, Stockholm: Natur & Kultur, 1993, pp. 52, 95.

21 Alun Howkins, 'The Discovery of Rural England' in Robert Colls and Philip Dodd (eds), *Englishness. Politics and Culture 1880–1920* (London: Croom Helm, 1986), pp. 62–88.

22 At that time, a people's temperament was considered as something inherited in a nation or a geographical district in Sweden, for example, the book *Det svenska folklynnet* (1911) was widely circulated and was important in maintaining that a love of nature was inherent to the Swede. Gustav Sundbärg, *Det svenska folklynnet* (Stockholm: Norstedts, 1911).

23 *Marketing Communication* 2010, p. 46 (IHA).

24 Christer Nordlund, 'Att lära känna sitt land och sig själv. Aspekter på konstitueringen av det svenska nationallandskapet' in Per Eliasson and Ebba Lisberg Jensen (eds), *Naturens nytta* (Lund: Historiska Media, 2000), pp. 20–59.

25 The description appears under the heading 'Swedish Heritage' on IKEA's website: http://www. ikea.com/ms/en_GB/about_ikea/the_ikea_way/swedish_heritage/index.html (accessed October 10, 2013). Basically identical formulations regarding nature are also spread internally, see *Our Way* 2008, *Our Way Forward* 2011 (IHA).

26 Olle Larsson, Lennart Johansson and Lars-Olof Larsson, *Smålands historia* (Lund: Historia Media, 2006).

27 *Our Way Forward* 2011, p. 45 (IHA).

28 Former CEO Anders Dahlvig interviewed and quoted in Wigerfelt 2012, p. 31.

29 The description appears on IKEA's website under the heading 'Swedish Heritage/Swedish Society': http://www.ikea.com/ms/en_GB/about_ikea/the_ikea_way/swedish_heritage/index. html (accessed October 10, 2013).

30 Yvonne Hirdman: *Vi bygger landet. Den svenska arbetarrörelsens historia från Per Götrek till Olof Palme*, Stockholm: Tidens förlag, Stockholm, 1990 (2nd ed.), pp. 282–4.

31 Marquis W. Childs, *Sweden. The Middle Way* (New Haven: Yale, 1936).

32 Per Albin Hansson gave his speech in the Swedish parliament's second chamber in 1928. For a survey of Swedish history between the years 1920 and 1965, and the first historical summary of the Swedish welfare state, see Yvonne Hirdman, Jenny Björkman and Urban Lundberg (eds), *Sveriges Historia 1920–1965* (Stockholm: Nordstedts, 2012).

33 Hirdman, Björkman and Lundberg 2012; Jenny Andersson, *När framtiden redan hänt. Socialdemokratin och folkhemsnostalgin* (Stockholm: Ordfront, 2009).

34 *Democratic Design. A Book About Form, Function and Price—Three Dimensions at IKEA* (Inter IKEA Systems B.V., 1995), p. 9 (IHA).

35 Maria Göransdotter, 'Smakfostran och heminredning. Om estetiska diskurser och bildning till bättre boende i Sverige 1930–1955' in Johan Söderberg and Lars Magnusson (eds), *Kultur och konsumtion i Norden 1750–1950* (Helsingfors: FHS, 1997).

36 Ellen Key, 'Beauty in the Home' [1899] in Lucy Creagh, Helena Kåberg and Barbara Miller Lane (eds), *Modern Swedish Design. Three Founding Texts* (New York: Museum of Modern Art, 2008), pp. 33–55.

37 Key 2008, p. 35.

38 Key 2008, pp. 43–4.

39 Description on IKEA's website under the heading 'Swedish Heritage.' http://www.ikea.com/ms/
en_GB/about_ikea/the_ikea_way/swedish_heritage/index.html (accessed October 10, 2013).
Also instructive is the fact that IKEA sponsored a major exhibition of the Larssons shown at the
Victoria & Albert in London 1997: *Carl and Karin Larsson. Creators of the Swedish Style*.
Werner 2008:2, p. 374.

40 Ellen Key, 'The Education of the Child' [1900, 1909], reprinted from the authorized English
translation of 'The Century of the Child'; with introductory note by Edward Bok (New York: G. P.
Putnamn's Sons, 1912). During the 1930s and the 1940s the concepts of family policy and a
free upbringing became accepted in Sweden. See Kerstin Vinterhed, *Gustav Jonsson på Skå.
En epok i svensk barnavård*, Diss. (Stockholm: Tiden, 1977), p. 209.

41 On Gregor Paulsson and his activities from 1915 to 1925 see Gunnela Ivanov, *Vackrare
vardagsvara—design för alla?: Gregor Paulsson och Svenska slöjdföreningen 1915–1925*,
Diss., Umeå: Umeå university, Department of Historical Studies, 2004). The functionalist ideas
primarily found expression in the new housing shown at the Stockholm Exhibition and by no
means everyone was positive about the new ideas and aesthetic. There was a rancorous
debate ('Slöjdstriden') in conjunction with the exhibition between Paulsson and Carl Malmsten.
See Eva Rudberg, *Stockholmsutställningen 1930. Modernismens genombrott i svensk
arkitektur* (Stockholm: Stockholmania, 1999); Eva Eriksson, *Den moderna staden tar form.
Arkitektur och debatt 1919–1935* (Stockholm: Ordfront, 2001).

42 Gunnar Asplund, Wolter Gahn, Sven Markelius, Eskil Sundahl and Uno Åhrén, 'acceptera'
[1931] in Creagh, Kåberg and Barbara Miller Lane 2008. The book was published on the Social
Democrats' own imprint, Tiden, and the leader of the Social Democrats, Per Albin Hansson,
moved into a functionalist terrace house designed by Paul Hedqvist. There is a great deal of
research concerning Swedish modernist architecture and housing policy. See Eriksson 2001;
Rudberg 1999. Swedish modernism is generally portrayed as a softer middle way. More
recently it has been claimed that Swedish modernism was a rather rigid and uncompromising
ideological cornerstone, a sort of mutual understanding between labor and capital. See Helena
Mattsson and Sven-Olof Wallenstein, *1930/1931. Den svenska modernismen vid vägskälet =
Swedish Modernism at the Crossroads = Der Schwedische Modernismus am Scheideweg*
(Stockholm: Axl Books, 2009).

43 All the texts are available in English translation with comments in Creagh, Kåberg and Miller
Lane 2008.

44 Gotthard Johansson (ed.), *Bostadsvanor och bostadsnormer* [Bostadsvanor i Stockholm under
1940-talet]/Svenska Arkitekters Riksförbund och Svenska Slöjdföreningens Bostadsutredning
(Stockholm: Kooperativa Förbundets förlag, 1964) [1955].

45 Göransdotter 1997; Lasse Brunnström, *Svensk designhistoria* (Stockholm: Raster, 2010).

46 Description on IKEA's hemsida under rubriken 'Swedish Heritage.' http://www.ikea.com/ms/
en_GB/about_ikea/the_ikea_way/swedish_heritage/index.html (accessed October10, 2013).

47 NK's interior designs and displays were a major source of inspiration when IKEA introduced its
room settings at the end of the 1960s. Lena Larsson was the artistic director at NK-bo and
was later awarded a prize by IKEA. Interview with Ekmark 2011; On Lena Larsson and the
NK-bo operation see Lena Larsson, *Varje människa är ett skåp* (Stockholm: Trevi, 1991).

48 Werner 2008:2, p. 345.

49 The exhibition and its significance is addressed in several articles in Halén and Wickman 2003.
See, in particular, Claire Selkurt, 'Design for a Democracy,' pp. 59–65; Harri Kalha, 'Just One of
Those Things,' pp. 67–75.

50 Kalha, 'Just One of Those Things' in Halén and Wickman 2003, p. 70.

51 Selkurt, 'Design for a Democracy' in Halén and Wickman 2003, p. 63.

52 Harri Kalha, 'The Other Modernism: Finnish Design and National Identity' in Marianne Aav and Nina Stritzler-Levine (eds), *Finnish Modern Design. Utopian Ideals and Everyday realities, 1930–1997* (New Haven: Yale University Press, 1998), pp. 29–51.

53 Ulf Hård af Segerstad, *Scandinavian Design* (Stockholm: Nord, 1962), p. 7.

54 Denise Hagströmer, 'An Experiment's Indian Summer. The Formes Scandinaves Exhibition' in Halén and Wickman 2003, p. 93.

55 Brunnström 2010, p. 14; Werner 2008:2, pp. 343–6.

56 On Ekmark's position within IKEA see note 141, chapter 2.

57 Before the term 'Living Situations' was coined the expression 'Livet Hemma' [Life at home] was used. Interview with Lennart Ekmark, Lea Kumpulainen, Range Strategist, June 12, 2009; 'Livet Hemma.' Document given to the author by Lennart Ekmark. Undated.

58 Interview with Ekmark, Lea Kumpulainen, 2009.

59 In spite of the 'global' guidelines there are local variations. For example, bed measurements in the USA have been aligned with US king and queen sizes while wardrobe fittings differ in that Americans prefer to store clothes folded up, while Italians, for example, use hangers. Interview with Intervju Ekmark, Lea Kumpulainen, 2009; Atle Bjarnestam 2009, pp. 205–9; Dahlvig 2011, pp. 94–7.

60 Atle Bjarnestam 2009, pp. 205–9; Dahlvig 2011, pp. 94–7.

61 *The IKEA Concept*, 2011, p. 24. This is repeated in numerous manuals. See also Dahlvig 2011, pp. 94–7.

62 Interview with Ekmark, Lea Kumpulainen, 2009; Atle Bjarnestam 2009, pp. 205–9; Dahlvig 2011, pp. 94–7.

63 Brunnström 2010, p. 352. There is also an account of the importance of the standardized pallet in the IKEA display *IKEA Explore* (IKCC).

64 Interview with Ekmark, Lea Kumpulainen, 2009; Atle Bjarnestam 2009, pp. 205–9.

65 The system was developed by Lennart Ekmark. Interview with Ekmark, Lea Kumpulainen, 2009; Atle Bjarnestam 2009, pp. 205–9; Ekmark interviewed in Bengtsson 2009. Unpaginated catalog.

66 Interview with Ekmark, Lea Kumpulainen, 2009; Atle Bjarnestam 2009, pp. 205–9; Ekmark interviewed in Bengtsson 2009. Unpaginated catalog.

67 A survey of IKEA's manuals shows that the various styles have changed names over the years. These four groups can be regarded as principal headings. See also Atle Bjarnestam 2009, pp. 205–9. In 2012 the four stylistic groups were called *Scandinavian Traditional, Scandinavian Modern, Popular Modern, Popular Traditional*. These, in turn, had subgroups. *Insight, IKEA IDEAS*, March 2012, Issue 87 (Inter IKEA Systems B.V., 2012) (IHA).

68 Interview with Ekmark, Lea Kumpulainen, 2009; Atle Bjarnestam 2009, pp. 205–9; Stenebo 2009, pp. 107–8.

69 Stenebo 2009.

70 The range has included products by, for example, Tapio Wirkkala, Vico Magistretti and Verner Panton. Kerstin Wickman, 'A Furniture Store for Everyone' in Bengtsson 2009. Unpaginated catalog.

71 A noted example is IKEA's collaboration with Hella Jongerius. That the limelight has been increasingly directed at designers is also noted in Wickman, 'A Furniture Store for Everyone' in Bengtsson 2009. Unpaginated catalog.

72 *Scandinavian Collections 1996–97*, DVD (Inter IKEA Systems B.V., 1997); *Stockholm* (Inter IKEA Systems B.V., 1996); *1700-tal* (Inter IKEA Systems B.V., 1996); *PS* (Inter IKEA Systems B.V., 1996) (IHA).

73 Lennart Ekmark interviewed in *Scandinavian Collections* 1997 (IHA).

74 *Vackrare vardag* (Inter IKEA Systems, B.V., Produced by Brindfors, 1990) (IHA).

75 *Vackrare vardag* (Inter IKEA Systems, B.V., Produced by Brindfors, 1990) (IHA).

76 IKEA collaborated with Lars Sjöberg, expert on eighteenth century style and keeper at the Nationalmuseum in Stockholm. *Svenskt 1700-tal på IKEA i samarbete med Riksantikvarieämbetet* (Älmhult: Inter IKEA Systems/Riksantikvarieämbetet, 1993).

77 In certain cases, manufacturing was adapted to contemporary production conditions. Because of strict environmental rules it was not possible to paint furniture using linseed-oil paints which are mixed with thinners. Instead, water-based paints were used. Elisabet Stavenow-Hidemark, 'IKEA satsar på svenskt 1700-tal,' *Hemslöjden*, Nr. 5 (1993), pp. 31–3.

78 *1700-tal* 1996, p. 3 (IHA).

79 The collection was a success with the media and attracted international attention. An analysis can be found in Susan Howe, 'Untangling the Scandinavian Blonde. Modernity and the IKEA PS Range Catalog 1995,' *Scandinavian Journal of Design*, No. 9 (1999), pp. 94–105.

80 Lennart Ekmark was in charge of the project together with consultant Stefan Ytterborn. Ekmark reports on the collection in *Scandinavian Collections* 1997. Ytterborn gives an account of the collaboration in Raul Cabra and Katherine E. Nelson (eds), *New Scandinavian Design* (San Francisco: Chronicle Books, 2004), pp. 48–52. Since 1995, other PS collections have been launched on themes such as 'Barnens PS' [Children's PS].

81 Howe 1999, p. 94.

82 *IKEA PS. Forum för design* (text by Kerstin Wickman) (Älmhult, IKEA of Sweden, 1995).

83 Lis Hogdal, 'Demokratisk design och andra möbler,' *Arkitektur*, No. 4 (1995), pp. 64–7.

84 See, for example, Ulf Beckman, 'Dags för design,' *Form*, Nr. 2 (1995), pp. 44–9.

85 Howe 1999, p. 104.

86 Slogan (1956) quoted in Werner 2008:2, p. 185.

87 During the 1960s references to Sweden were replaced by more generalized allusions to the Nordic countries. That the national markers retired to the background does not necessarily mean that Volvo no longer had anything to win from being linked with Sweden. By this time the car manufacturer's Swedish origins may have become self-evident while in marketing there was a general view that the country of origin did not need to be emphasized. Werner 2008:2, pp. 187–90. See also Christina Zetterlund, *Design i informationsåldern. Om strategisk design, historia och praktik*, Diss. (Stockholm: Raster, 2002), pp. 72–3.

88 Anonymous designer quoted in Werner 2008:2, p. 192. The quotation is from Toni-Matti Karjalainen: *Semantic Transformation in Design. Communication Strategic Brand Idenitity Through Product Design References*, Diss. (Helsinki: University of Art and Design, 2004); Zetterlund 2002, p. 73.

89 In 1991 Peter Horbury from the UK was appointed chief designer at Volvo. Alongside Horbury, Mexican José de la Vega was also influential in the changes that gave Volvo a more Scandinavian image. Werner 2008:2, pp. 194–6.

90 Even SAS's former profile used Scandinavian markers. For example, the logotype alluded to the colors of the Swedish, Norwegian and Danish flags. Eva Hemmungs Wirtén, Susanna Skarrie Wirtén, *Föregångarna. Design management i åtta svenska företag* (Stockholm: Informationsförlaget, 1989), pp. 64–5. On SAS's design program in the 1990s see Tyler Brûlé, 'Blondes do it Better,' *Wallpaper*, No. 14 (1998), pp. 101–4; Marie-Louise Bowallius and Michael Toivio, 'Mäktiga märken' in Lena Holger and Ingalill Holmberg (eds), *Identitet. Om varumärken, tecken och symboler* (Stockholm: Raster, 2002), pp. 18–19.

91 Denise Hagströmer, *Swedish Design* (Stockholm: Swedish Institute, 2001), p. 116; Jelena Zetterström, 'Hjärnorna bakom SAS nya ansikte,' *Dagens industri*, May 21, 2001.

92 Photo of baggage train in an article on the design program, Ola Andersson, 'Saker som får oss att vilja röka crack: SAS nya designprofil,' *Bibel*, Nr. 5 (1999).

93 Magdalena Petersson, *Identitetsföreställningar. Performance, normativitet och makt ombord på SAS och AirHoliday*, Diss. (Göteborg: Mara, 2003).

94 Carl Hamilton, *Historien om flaskan* (Stockholm: Norstedts, 1994); Richard W. Lewis, *Absolut Book. The Absolut Vodka Advertising Story* (Boston, Mass: Journey Editions, 1996).

95 Wickman, 'A Furniture Store for Everyone' in Bengtsson 2009. Unpaginated catalog; Atle Bjarnestam 2009, pp. 73–82.

96 *Designed for People. Swedish Home Furnishing 1700–2000* (Inter IKEA Systems B.V., 1999), p. 17.

97 Eva Londos, *Uppåt väggarna. En etnologisk studie av bildbruk*, Diss. (Stockholm: Carlsson/ Jönköping Läns Museum, 1993), pp. 179–81.

98 Interview with product developer at IKEA with responsibility for purchasing images, in Oivvio Polite, 'Global hissmusik på var mans vägg,' *Dagens Nyheter*, October 23, 2004.

99 This project is described by Wigerfelt 2012. The campaign was also noted by Dahlvig 2011, pp. 59–62.

100 Headings quoted by Wigerfelt 2012, pp. 23–4.

4
SWEDEN DESIGNED BY IKEA

The film *Sweden—Open Skies, Open Minds* (2007) portrays a contented country in northern Europe with a perfect mix of beautiful countryside, modern industry and cultural heritage (Figure 4.1). Rapid changes of scene from people diving from rugged cliffs in the archipelago, children playing, grazing cows, corn fields, and country estates are mixed with nightclubs, fashion shows and manufacturing pharmaceuticals. In certain shots dark-skinned people hurry past among all the blue-eyed blonds like politically correct alibis: Sweden is a country of diversity and openness.[1]

This is an official film promoting Sweden's image, produced by an advertising agency on a commission from the Swedish Institute, which is the Swedish body responsible for monitoring and improving Sweden's image abroad.[2] The genre is that of the advertising film and *Sweden—Open Skies, Open Minds* can be seen as a form of nation branding, which is hardly concerned with problematizing issues or bringing visibility to complications. The genre is more interested in promoting powerful and attractive images of a country in order to profile it on a global market. It is, in other words, a matter of making oneself cosmetically more attractive in order to strengthen one's competitive edge.

Countries have long employed a variety of methods to create a positive buzz about them as nations. But in recent decades they have increasingly borrowed vocabulary and tools from the marketing sphere and this chapter accordingly discusses how Sweden makes use of IKEA, looking at the importance of the company in Sweden's own nation branding.

IKEA has long sold interior furnishings beneath a blue and yellow flag with the help of established notions about Swedish society (Plate 15). Now, in the twenty-first century, the roles seem to have been mutually exchanged. The fact that IKEA's products are not manufactured in Sweden and that the concept is owned by a foundation in the Netherlands is of less importance in this context. IKEA plays an important role for 'Sweden,' that is to say, for the national brand. The opinion of the Swedish Institute is that: 'Frankly, IKEA is doing more to disseminate the image of Sweden than all governmental efforts put together.'[3]

The brand state

A common view at the end of the last century was that the nation, as such, was losing ground as globalization increased. But developments took a different direction. The threat to the nation state seems, rather, to have caused a sort of cultural backlash in its defense.

The film *Sweden — Open Skies, Open Minds* takes you on an exciting, high-speed journey from north to south, east to west and back again — racing across blue skies, over vast landscapes and open seas, into the vibrant urbanity exploding with creativity, meeting people of all ages and origins, face-to-face with Sweden of today.

Length: 4.33 minutes

Produced by the Council for the Promotion of Sweden and the Swedish Institute (www.si.se).

The Swedish Institute (SI) is a public agency that promotes interest in Sweden abroad. SI seeks to establish cooperation and lasting relations with other countries through active communication and cultural, educational and scientific exchanges. SI works closely with Swedish embassies and consulates around the world.

Sweden.se, the country's official gateway, is a rich source of information that provides a direct insight into contemporary Sweden in many different languages.

SI.
Swedish Institute | *Sharing Sweden with the world*

Figure 4.1 'Open Skies, Open Minds.' An official film promoting Sweden's image, produced by the agency BrittonBritton. (© BrittonBritton, Stockholm.)

This may seem contradictory but globalization and nationalism do not necessarily have to exclude each other, and the way in which nationalism expresses itself varies over time.

In recent decades various countries have worked more or less strategically to market themselves as nations and, in this context, ordinary commercial brands are important. This was pointed out by Peter van Ham in an article entitled *The Rise of the Brand State* (2001) which is frequently quoted: '. . . in many ways, Microsoft and McDonald's are among the most visible US diplomats, just as Nokia is Finland's envoy to the world . . . Strong brands are important in attracting foreign direct investment, recruiting the best and the brightest, and wielding political influence.'[4]

As long ago as 1996 Simon Anholt invented a tool to measure a country's strength as a brand. By asking thousands of people in a succession of countries about how they view other countries he manages to establish a value as to the status of the country as a brand. The national brand is not, of course, a product as we normally understand the term, and it is not a question of what is produced in a specific country, but of how the country is perceived. For many Europeans, for example, it seems more natural to holiday in France or Italy than in Latvia, a country which has both sandy beaches and cultural artifacts but no strong holidaying tradition. And, as a country formerly in the eastern bloc, Latvia still enjoys low status; that is to say, it needs more marketing if it is to attract visitors.

Accordingly, nation branding builds on the idea that states do not just have a political agenda but that they are also responsible for a brand. The point is that countries carry meanings and are charged with significances. Numerous variables are involved. Among the positive elements are famous people and well-known tourist attractions.[5] Briefly, marketing a country is just like the usual forms of advertising, a matter of creating and launching attractive images and narratives. It is a question of supporting the business sector and increasing growth: attracting tourists, investors, skilled employees and trading partners. That is to say, it is a matter of launching the nation just as one would a new lipstick or a line of sports shoes.

The same principle applies to cities or geographical regions which are now involved in 'city branding' or 'place branding.' But local slogans and the hunt for visitors and investors have a history that stretches back for many decades. One well-known example is New

York City which, in the mid-1970s, had a bad reputation: increasing waves of crime and exhaust fumes discouraged people from visiting the city. But in 1977 a successful campaign was launched, 'I Love New York,' commissioned by the city authorities as a way of restoring the city's lost honor.[6]

Stockholm, the capital of Sweden, has also worked to promote its brand. The city has chosen the slogan 'The Capital of Scandinavia' and the arrival hall at Arlanda International Airport features a display entitled 'Stockholm Hall of Fame' which is a cavalcade of photographs of Swedish celebrities. This is, of course, part of a highly conscious strategy, for the airport is where people meet Sweden for the first time and so the associations people make there are important.[7]

Nation branding can be seen as part of what Joseph Nye calls 'soft power.' While hard power is traditionally concerned with the military and with financial power, 'soft power' is about attracting and winning sympathy and seeming to be appealing; using, for example, design, attractive narratives and culture. In a global political context, according to Nye, it is a matter of combining soft and hard power in a fruitful manner, which is well illustrated by the US post-war policy in Europe.[8]

From this perspective, Marshall aid can be seen as a form of soft power. The money was used for rebuilding Europe as well as for trying to persuade Europeans as to the advantages of democracy and the market economy. But it also meant a flood wave of culture from the USA that sponsored exhibitions and films, for example, and also gave considerable financial support to design schools like the Hochschule für Gestaltung in Ulm. The cold war was about nuclear weapons, the arms race and landing on the moon, but equally important were consumerism, culture and attractive everyday products.[9]

One notable example of a country that has worked hard at improving its brand is Spain. In the mid-1970s Spain was a poor and relatively remote part of Europe. The country was associated with fascism, with Franco and with repression but it was successful in changing this image over quite a brief period. One important step in this process was represented by a tourist campaign in 1982 which included a symbol, a cheerful red sun, created by the painter Joan Miró. Instead of being linked with military rule and a dictatorship, Spain wanted to be associated with sunny beaches, art and Rioja wines.[10]

The British New Labour party's attempt to rebrand the UK is another pertinent example. In the mid-1990s it was claimed that foreigners associated the UK with royalty, buttered scones, gardening, English butlers and University of Oxford. The British identity, it was claimed, needed a good dusting. Rather than being considered conservative and tradition-bound, the country wanted to signal a young and creative nation. A well-oiled marketing machine was rolled into action to launch the slogan 'A Brand New Britain.' The project, named 'Cool Britannia' made particular use of design, fashion and art as strategic tools.[11] That youthfully hip sectors were prioritized at the expense of the traditional manufacturing and export industries gave rise to a good deal of criticism, however.[12]

Thus, nation branding is a controversial and much debated phenomenon and some scholars maintain that we should be careful not to overestimate the role of marketing activities in this regard. The Spanish success, for example, can also be explained by fundamental political and economic reforms.[13] And critics have asked whether it is possible, or even sensible, to market a country that is poor and is also fighting a war.[14] The field of nation branding often suffers from stereotyped notions about who we are and what defines us as a people and a nation. And, from a historical perspective, the strategy can also be understood as propaganda and an attempt to smooth over negative images. True, the marketing of countries today is not concerned with launching doctrines or religious ideas, but even dictatorships and autocratic leaders have made diligent use of marketing strategies and visual narratives in order to put their message across.

This is, at any rate, the view of Steven Heller in his book *Iron Fists: Branding the 20th Century Totalitarian State* (2011) in which he demonstrates how dictators in the Soviet Union, in communist China, in Mussolini's Italy and in Nazi Germany have presented their policies with the help of design and the use of narratives. The title of the book indicates similarities with business strategies and politics, an analogy that may seem somewhat unreasonable. But the point is that visual staging and choreography are essential regardless of whether one is trying to inculcate political doctrines or to increase sales of a commercial product. In Heller's perspective the difference between marketing products and ideas is minimal.[15]

Hitler, for example, was influenced by the German electrical engineering firm AEG's design program created by Peter Behrens back in the 1910s. Like Behrens, using graphic design, products and factories, Hitler produced carefully thought-out manuals describing fonts, symbols and flags. And just like Mussolini, Mao and Stalin, Hitler functioned as a sort of logotype himself. The different leaders chose different elements and their images are different, but Heller maintains that the brand-building process has a common denominator.

There is similar criticism of the marketing of cities and locations. As early as the 1980s David Harvey minted the term entrepreneurialism in urban governance. Put simply, Harvey maintains that those involved in urban governance today see themselves as businessmen whose job it is to ensure that the city is competitive. During the 1980s the city of Baltimore, where Harvey was based, underwent a complete transformation from a manufacturing city in crisis to a lively tourist metropolis. But there was also a downside to the transformation: a sort of division between places visited by thousands of tourists and the rest of the city which was characterized by social deprivation and slum dwellings. According to Harvey, politics in the entrepreneurial city is mainly about improving the business climate and attracting investment rather than redistributing resources and administering welfare.[16]

In spite of the criticism directed at nation branding, all countries are more or less consciously concerned with marketing themselves.[17] One common view is that there is a built-in inertia in the process. Nation branding cannot be used as a quick fix for eradicating a negative impression since how a country is perceived is based on notions that are deeply embedded and that cannot be changed overnight.

Brand Sweden

New Labour and Tony Blair's tactics almost certainly had an influence on Swedish politicians. It was not long before the Swedish minister, Leif Pagrotsky, was seen wearing dark glasses in the company of the then internationally famous rock band Cardigans, while he furnished his office with new Swedish design. Pagrotsky was one of the politicians who regularly stressed the importance of design for the business sector, arguing that design could be used to produce an attractive and appealing image of Sweden.[18]

Efforts to build the national brand accelerated after the turn of the millennium with the Swedish Institute leading the way in collaboration with other bodies.[19] That the country has long enjoyed a good reputation and that the media function as messengers was of great importance in this respect. In 1998 the British lifestyle magazine *Wallpaper* selected Sweden as the world's design capital and it is claimed that editor Tyler Brûlé's love of the Swedish capital was more important in promoting the brand than all the official marketing efforts. Similar importance attaches to *Newsweek*'s cover and special issue devoted to Stockholm and Sweden as the information society's spearhead which was published two years later.[20]

In 2005 Sweden came out top of the Anholt Nation Brands Index. The ranking was seen as reflecting the importance of security and order in an unstable world.[21] Whether the people interviewed for the index really knew anything about the country is not clear. It seems unlikely that they would have been able to name any Swedish politicians or even to point out Sweden on the map. Thus the positive view of Sweden was hardly the result of a concrete knowledge of the country but should rather be regarded as the fruit of deeply rooted notions about the country.[22]

With a view to maintaining its lofty position on the chart, advertising agencies and public relations (PR) consultants were taken on board and, in 2007, the Swedish brand was launched with its key values: Innovative, Open, Authentic, Caring. These were summarized in turn as Progressive.[23] The term 'Open' denotes: '. . . freedom of thought and diversity between people, cultures and lifestyles.'[24] One concrete example is the principle of open government and open justice which gives everyone the right to consult public documents and to attend courts of law and political forums. The key value 'Authentic' is explained as: '. . . being natural and unpretentious. It projects itself in reliability, honesty and informality: simple and clear.'[25] The concept is illustrated with the claim that all Swedes have a close relationship with nature: 'northern Europe's last wilderness.'[26]

'Caring' is defined as: 'Thoughtfulness is the consideration of every individual. Safety and security are important, similarly the respect and inclusion of everyone. A wish to learn from people and nature, to meet the needs of others and to feel empathy.'[27] 'Innovative' means the ability to see things in a new light: 'Sweden has unique design, fashion and popular culture. But also a modern harmonious lifestyle, sensitivity to trends and world-leading research.'[28]

On the government website Sweden.se — 'The official gateway to Sweden' — the image of Sweden is disseminated with the help of numerous photographs of lakes and forest horizons, happy children and smiling old-age pensioners. Besides clichés about Swedes being a nature-loving people the country is portrayed as consciously modern, a paradise for both tourists and investors.[29] The branding project seems to be about maintaining the fiction that this is a homogeneous society and a national 'we.' It is Swedish values, lifestyle and way of thinking that are to be marketed.

In building Sweden's national brand, as we have noted, design has been considered an important tool for providing an attractive image. But not by any means all design: 'Function, not decoration, is the framework of what could be called the typical Swedish design creed.'[30] In 2005 the Swedish government announced a *Design Year* with the Ministry of Enterprise deeply involved and proudly explaining that the success of Swedish design was due to: 'pure, carefully considered and innovative forms.'[31] That a nation and its people should embrace a particular style is a dated notion. But, in practice, the concept was clearly included, for in launching Sweden as a brand it was primarily a stripped-down, functional, and even blond form that was considered best suited for expressing the nation.

Clearly there are common denominators between Sweden's national brand and IKEA's own brand. It is very evident that a sense of solidarity, security and equality are identified as central aspects both of the national brand and of IKEA's own brand. And both brands emphasize a type of design that is light and unornamented. The images and narratives of Swedish design harmonize with each other and it is not difficult to understand why Swedish ministries concerned with promoting the Swedish brand should consider IKEA as a significant player in the game.

Sweden loves IKEA

The Swedish Institute's view of IKEA's importance to the national brand is clear: 'To visit IKEA is to visit Sweden. IKEA fits very well onto the official brand platform of Sweden. The company has been at the forefront of corporate social responsibility, putting stress on the working conditions of their contractors as well as on sustainability. The brand of the company could very well be described in the same terms as the platform for Sweden.'[32] There are similar reference points and the furniture company comes to be regarded as a sort of ally: 'It goes both ways: Sweden benefits from the way IKEA markets itself. But IKEA is one of the companies that most benefit from the image of Sweden. IKEA would not be IKEA without its Swedish background.'[33]

The Swedish authorities' view of IKEA is illuminating. In discussions about the contribution of the business sector in promoting the Swedish national brand, the spotlight is on IKEA. A government report from 2011 concluded: 'Certain major Swedish corporations like IKEA and Volvo Cars have long made use of their Swedish origins in their marketing. As a result of the enormous resources that help to promote Sweden as a brand, Sweden is widely associated precisely with these companies (despite the fact that Volvo Cars has not been a Swedish-owned company for the last ten years). The value to the Swedish image that these companies contribute with their marketing can scarcely be calculated.[34]

The rhetoric could just as well have come from an advertising agency. By means of what is known as cross-branding or co-branding the state seeks to capitalize on other brands that are already established. Another government report (2004) recommends basically merging with a number of brands: 'Co-branding and making joint use of activities with the major international Swedish corporations is an effective way of gaining a great deal from very limited funding for marketing and brand building on the part of the authorities. Locally, when IKEA opens a new store, this can create a natural opportunity for linking up with an activity that promotes Sweden . . .'[35]

Calculating the importance of IKEA to how people perceive Sweden is a complex task. IKEA is established in a large number of countries throughout the world and the actual reception varies from place to place, depending on a country's different cultural, social and economic status. Many people probably experience the product names and the food as exotic. In some countries IKEA is seen as the model of a budget-price store while in others it is perceived as progressive from a design aspect. However, one can find out just what the Swedish foreign missions think about IKEA's role in the host country. Embassies and consulates literally represent Sweden and their operations include activities, projects and collaborative ventures that aim at promoting Sweden as a brand.

In 2010, Sweden's embassies and consulates were asked to present proposals for improving the national brand. The proposals contain an introductory and general account of the host country's image of Sweden. The introduction is followed by a list of ideas about possible projects and wishes for collaboration with business partners, for example. The more than eighty promotional propositions speak clearly: to a large extent the authorities regard IKEA as Sweden's face in the world and the company gains a remarkably prominent place in the reports. Perceptions of Sweden and Swedes vary, of course, from country to country. Generally speaking the associations are positive and, in most cases, the images are linked to concepts like social welfare, justice and equality.

The report from Russia is instructive: 'Sweden is associated with honesty, quality, the third-way good society ['third-way' means neither a Socialistic or capitalistic society], modernity, neutrality and, perhaps, a degree of affinity.'[36] From Lisbon, too, the reaction is positive: 'The image of Sweden is of a prosperous country where there is social justice, a well-developed economy and where there is concern for the environment.'[37] Generally speaking the Swedish authorities set great store by the leading companies and if IKEA is represented there it is almost always regarded as a good representative of Sweden and a useful partner. The Swedish embassy in Singapore opined: 'In the business sector, IKEA often has to shoulder the responsibility of representing Sweden. . . .'[38] And in Iceland they maintain that IKEA is 'the flagship when it comes to a visible presence.'[39] The embassy in Greece notes that: 'IKEA currently has four blue and yellow stores . . . which provide good PR for Sweden.'[40] The report from Israel also mentions the IKEA stores: 'On the positive side, there is a view that Sweden produces quality products (Volvo, IKEA, H&M, etc.). . . .'[41] If IKEA is not established in a country but plans to start up there, this is noted by the embassy staff. From Thailand the embassy reports: 'In conjunction with IKEA opening the first (of several) stores in Thailand on 3 November 2011, we see opportunities for exploiting the Swedish brand more widely.'[42] The Jordanian embassy notes that it 'regularly gets asked by people in Jordan about IKEA's possible plans for opening a store in the country.'[43] In Belgrade, too, there is great interest in an IKEA store that is currently planned. The embassy is collaborating with IKEA which has also donated SEK 400,000–500,000 for sponsorship.[44]

The general opinion is that the company's profile corresponds to a currently positive perception of Sweden (Figure 4.2). IKEA stands for things that Sweden wants to be

Monsieur le Président, nous savons que le modèle suédois vous fascine, mais pourquoi aller si loin?

TIMMERMAN - Pin massif. Vernis incolore.
Module : larg. 70 Prof. 37 cm
L'ensemble présenté : **4320**F

Monsieur le Président, à vous qui partez en Suède, nous souhaitons bon voyage d'heureuses rencontres et de nombreuses découvertes. Mais savez-vous qu'il vous suffisait d'aller à Evry, Bobigny et Lyon pour connaître le mode de vie suédois?

Là, chez IKEA, vous auriez pu admirer les dernières créations des designers de Suède. Les meubles et tous les objets qui font la vie quotidienne des suédois. Vous auriez remarqué que ce mode de vie a du bon puisque tous les modèles IKEA ne

sont pas seulement de bonne qualité et agréables à vivre. Ils ont un charme supplémentaire indéniable : leur bas prix.
Et cela grâce à la participation des clients qui montent leurs meubles eux-mêmes.
Vive la participation, Monsieur le Président.

IKEA EVRY - AUTOROUTE DU SUD
SORTIE AIRE DE LISSES TEL. (6) 497.68.65.
Lun., Mar., Mer., Ven. : 11-20 h - Jeu. : 11-22 h -
Sam. : 9-20 h - Dim : 11-19 h.
📞 🍴 RESTAURANT - PARADIS D'ENFANTS

IKEA BOBIGNY. CENTRE COMMERCIAL BOBIGNY 2
TEL. (1) 832.92.95 (à 5 mn de la Porte de Pantin)
Lun., Mar., Mer. : 11-20 h - Jeu. et Ven. : 11-22 h - Samedi : 9-20 h

IKEA LYON. CENTRE COMMERCIAL DU GRAND VIRE.
VAULX-EN-VELIN. TEL. (7) 879.23.26.
Heures d'ouverture : Lun. - Vend. : 11-20 h - Samedi : 9-20 h

Ils sont fous ces Suédois

Figure 4.2 Ad, 'Monsieur le Président, nous savons que le modèle suédois vous fascine, mais pourquoi aller si loin' [Monsieur President, we know that the Swedish model fascinates you, but why go so far], 1982 or 1983. The man holding a red rose—a symbol of social democracy—is a look-alike of President Mitterrand and the whole advertisement alludes to the Swedish model. (Used with the permission of Inter IKEA Systems B.V. © Inter IKEA Systems B.V.)

associated with and so the company plays an important part in establishing a view of Sweden. That brands with a national profile to an extent function as images of the original country is entirely natural. Formally these brands do not represent the country, however, informally they do. And it is not just a matter of reflecting Sweden but also of reproducing perceptions.

Volvo, for example, has long alluded in its marketing to the image of Sweden as a country concerned with safety, but the company has also strengthened this perception. The manufacturing process is no longer Swedish and the cars consist of parts that are produced in other countries, while Volvo is actually owned by a Chinese firm. Nor are IKEA's products manufactured in Sweden but, in both cases, the national origin is important to the profile of the brand. The visual images, narratives and symbols that the companies disseminate influence the profile of the national brand and thus the image of Sweden. In this way the commercial actors help to shape notions about Swedish society and Swedish design. Thus companies do not just manufacture products but they mirror, reuse and reproduce national stereotypes and narratives. Regardless of one's view of exactly how 'Swedish' IKEA actually is, the company has, in various ways, influenced how Sweden and Swedishness have come to be perceived in other countries, as well as Sweden's own self-image.

Indeed there are many aspects of Swedish life that we can be proud of and there are many fine things worth displaying. But this does not exonerate us from reflecting on and monitoring these aspects of Swedish society. There is every reason to problematize and question both IKEA's and the Swedish Institute's images of and narratives about Sweden. What aspects are emphasized, which are the target groups, and who is responsible for the image, are questions that need to be discussed. Questioning and problematizing are not part of the brand strategist's normal task which is hardly concerned with revealing cracks in the national façade. The extent to which the perspectives of the Swedish brand, or of commercial brands, actually agree with reality is a different matter. Or as the Swedish Institute puts it: 'We are not concerned with how things are but how they are perceived.'[45]

Notes

1   The film was directed and produced by the firm BrittonBritton, commissioned by the Swedish Institute and the NSU (Committee for the Promotion of the Sweden Image Abroad, headed by the Foreign Ministry). From 2004, BrittonBritton worked with the Swedish Institute with the strategic and creative development of a new communicative platform for the official marketing of Sweden. The commission encompassed the creation of a visual concept, a new website launched in 2004, the development of the Image Bank Sweden, and the creation and production of the *Sweden&Swedes* booklet and theme website. Other units produced by BrittonBritton within the same project included the Sweden.se portable exhibition that toured at embassies, consulates and other venues worldwide. http://www.sweden.se/eng/Home/ Lifestyle/Visuals/Open-skies-open-minds/ (accessed June 13, 2013).

2   The Swedish Institute was founded in January 1945, tasked with promoting Sweden's cultural, social and economic links with other countries using publicity campaigns, cultural exchanges

and other methods. On the institute's history see Nikolas Glover, *National Relations. Public Diplomacy, National Identity and the Swedish Institute 1945–1970*, Diss. (Lund: Nordic Academic Press, 2011).

3 Olle Wästberg, 'The Lagging Brand of Sweden' in Kurt Almqvist and Alexander Linklater (eds), *Images of Sweden* (Stockholm: Axel and Margaret Ax:son Johnson Foundation, 2011), p. 141; Olle Wästberg, 'The Symbiosis of Sweden & IKEA,' *Public Diplomacy Magazine*, University of Southern California, Issue 2 (2009).

4 Peter van Ham, 'The Rise of the Brand State,' *Foreign Affairs*, Council of Foreign Relations, September/October (2001).

5 Much has been written on nation branding, not least in the consultants' own periodicals like *Public Diplomacy* and *Public Diplomacy Magazine* as well as in books like Simon Anholt, *Brand America. The Mother of All Brands* (London: Cyan, 2004); Simon Anholt, *Competitive Identity. The Brand Management for Nations, Cities and Regions* (New York: Palgrave Macmillan, 2007). For a more analytical sociological study see Melissa Aronczyk, *Branding the Nation: The Global Business of National Identity* (New York: Oxford University Press, 2013).

6 The graphic program for the campaign was created by Milton Glaser and is now regarded as emblematic of New York. See Milton Glaser: *Art is Work. Graphic Design, Objects and Illustration* (London: Thames & Hudson, 2000), p. 206.

7 The exhibition is the result of collaboration between Stockholm Arlanda Airport and Stockholm Business Region under the umbrella heading of The Capital of Scandinavia. For the history of Stockholm's self-image from the 1930s onwards, see Anna Kåring Wagman, *Stadens melodi. Information och reklam i Stockholms kommun 1930–1980*, Diss. (Stockholm: Stockholmia, 2006).

8 Nye 2004.

9 David Crowley and Jane Pavitt (eds), *Cold War Modern. Design 1945–1970* (London: V&A Publishing, 2008).

10 In the 1990s the image of Spain was further strengthened by the World Exhibition in Seville in 1992 and the Guggenheim Museum in Bilbao in 1997. Not to mention the Barcelona Olympics, the significance of which hinged on design. Teemu Moilanen and Seppo Rainisto, *How to Brand Nations, Cities and Destinations. A Planning Book for Place Branding* (Basingstoke: Palgrave Macmillan, 2009), pp. 5–6, 29, 72–3; Guy Julier, *The Culture of Design* (London: SAGE Publications, 2000), pp. 125–8.

11 Charlotte Werther, 'Cool Britannia, the Millennium Dome and the 2012 Olympics,' *Moderna Språk*, No. 11 (2011), pp. 1–14.

12 Ying Fan, 'Branding the nation: What is being branded?,' *Journal of Vacation Marketing*, Vol. 12, No. 1 (2006), pp. 5–14.

13 Fan 2006, p. 11.

14 Fan 2006, p. 13.

15 Steven Heller, *Iron Fists. Branding the 20th-century Totalitarian State* (London: Phaidon, 2008).

16 David Harvey, 'From Managerialism to Entrepreneurialism: The Transformation in Urban Governance in Late Capitalism,' *Geografiska Annaler. Series B, Human Geography*, Vol. 71, No. 1 (1989), pp. 3–17.

17 Ying Fan, 'Branding the nation. Towards a better understanding,' *Place Branding and Public Diplomacy*, Vol. 6 (2010), pp. 97–103.

18 See, for example, the speech by government minister Leif Pagrotsky: *Anförande näringsminister Leif Pagrotsky vid rådslaget för design i Stockholm den 15 Oktober 2003*. Government Offices of Sweden, http://www.regeringen.se/sb/d/1213/a/7499 (accessed June

1, 2013). Pagrotsky was Minister of Trade and Industry 2002–2004 and Minister of Culture 2004–2006.

19 Nämnden för Sverigefrämjande i utlandet (NSU) was established in 1995 with the aim of contributing to a clearer, more attractive and modern image of Sweden. The Swedish Institute collaborates with Invest in Sweden Agency, Exportrådet and Visit Sweden. http://www. regeringen.se/sb/d/3028 (accessed December 13, 2012).

20 Stryker McGuire, 'Shining Stockholm,' *Newsweek*, February 7, 2000.

21 This is Anholt's opinion based on their interpretation of the results of the study. Anholt Nation Brands Index Q1 2005. http://www.simonanholt.com/Publications/publications-other-articles. aspx (accessed June 1, 2013).

22 Anholt Nation Brands Index Q1 2005. http://www.simonanholt.com/Publications/publications-other-articles.aspx (accessed June 1, 2013).

23 Core values described at http://www.visitsweden.com/sweden/brandguide/The-brand/The Platform/Platform-Core-values/Open (accessed May 2, 2013).

24 http://www.visitsweden.com.

25 http://www.visitsweden.com.

26 http://www.visitsweden.com.

27 http://www.visitsweden.com.

28 http://www.visitsweden.com.

29 The website houses the archive 'Image Bank Sweden, produced by BrittonBritton. See note 1 of this chapter.

30 Wästberg 2009.

31 http://www.designaret.se/svensk-design/ (accessed June 1, 2013).

32 Wästberg, 'Images of Sweden,' in Almqvist and Linklater 2011, p. 141.

33 Wästberg 2009.

34 *Översyn av myndighetsstrukturen för Sverige-, handels- och investeringsfrämjande*, Departementserie 2011: 29, Utrikesdepartementet, Government Offices of Sweden, p. 123.

35 *Turistfrämjande för ökad tillväxt*, Statens offentliga utredningar, SOU 2004:17, Näringsdepartementet, Government Offices of Sweden p. 107.

36 *Främjandeplan Ryssland 2011–2013*, Sveriges Ambassad Moskva, Utrikesdepartementet Dnr. UF2010/69681/FIM, Kat: 4.5 (LMFA).

37 *Främjandeplan Lissabon 2011–2013*, Sveriges Ambassad Lissabon, Utrikesdepartementet, Dnr. UF2010/71903/FIM, Kat: 4.5 (LMFA).

38 *Främjandeplan Singapore 2011–2013*, Sveriges Ambassad Singapore, Utrikesdepartementet, Dnr. UF 2010/66401/FIM, Kat: 4.5 (LMFA).

39 *Främjandeplan för Island 2011–2013*, Sveriges Ambassad Reykjavik, Utrikesdepartementet, Dnr. UF 2010/66980/FIM: Kat, 4.5 (LMFA).

40 *Främjandeplan Grekland 2011–2013*, Sveriges Ambassad Athen, Utrikesdepartementet, Dnr. UF 2010/68981/FIM, Kat: 4.5 (LMFA).

41 *Främjandeplan Tel Aviv 2011–2013*, Sveriges Ambassad Tel Aviv, Utrikesdepartementet, Dnr. UF 2010/69971/FIM, Kat: 4.5 (LMFA).

42 *Främjandeplan Bangkok 2011–2013*, Sveriges Ambassad Bangkok, Utrikesdepartementet, Dnr. UF 2010/66885/FIM, Kat: 4.5 (LMFA).

43 *Främjandeplan 2011–2013, Sveriges Ambassad Amman*, Utrikesdepartementet, Dnr. UF 2010/68979/FIM, Kat: 4.5 (LMFA).

44 *Främjandeplan Belgrad 2011–2013*, Sveriges Ambassad Belgrad, Utrikesdepartementet, Dnr. UF 2010/68999/FIM, Kat: 4.5 (LMFA).

45 Quotation from seminar *Sverigebilden 2009—Varumärket Sverige och svenska företag i finanskrisen*, June 1, 2009. Quoted in Sara Kristoffersson, 'Reklamavbrott i må gott-fabriken,' *Svenska Dagbladet* June 10, 2009; Raoul Galli, *Varumärkenas fält. Produktion av erkännande i Stockholms reklamvärld*, Diss. (Stockholm: Acta Universitatis Stockholmiensis, 2012), p. 248.

5
COUNTER-NARRATIVES

Identifying a Swedish identity is a postmodern nightmare. Within Sweden's borders one finds different cultures, languages, lifestyles and social classes. With its multi-ethnicity and social heterogeneity it is not easy to establish any common denominators. But in the corporate world things seem a little less complicated. Branding strategies are not concerned with fine nuances or with demonstrating cracks in the façade, but with establishing as attractive and homogeneous an image as possible. This means that the images of Sweden that are launched by IKEA do not necessarily agree with other people's perceptions but represent the company's own image. Unemployment and sick leave do not figure in the company's narratives. In contrast to the idealized image communicated by IKEA there are portraits of Sweden that chafe.

Elsewhere in this book the importance of IKEA's own narratives has been discussed. In order to highlight their force it is necessary to relate to other narratives. The aim is not to falsify, counter or demolish the company's marketing but, rather, to study it in more detail and to understand how effective it is. IKEA is regarded as a global forerunner for Sweden and it does not just represent the country but also reproduces notions about Sweden; positively charged and established narratives about the country's welfare society and about Swedish design. These may be attractive and commercially successful, but they are also controversial since they are seriously widely challenged and are hardly in line with the times.

IKEA also describes itself as an innovative pioneer in several fields and this, too, can be questioned. In the present chapter, therefore, the aim is to survey and critically analyze the company's self-image. The focus will be the direct criticism that has been directed at IKEA and at how the company has dealt with this.

From social role model to brand

The perception of Sweden as a harmonious and secure welfare state is well-known and well established, even though divergent views can also be found. Conservative groups in the USA and the UK have portrayed Sweden as a sort of welfare dystopia, a semi-totalitarian 'nanny' state in which the authorities monitor and control the citizens. But it was not until the 1980s and 1990s that the image of Swedish society was seriously renegotiated and revised. There was a re-evaluation of the welfare state and critics began to look at the cracks in the façade and to discuss the negative aspects of Swedish society. This led to the success story about Sweden being successively rewritten.[1]

One example of this questioning of the Swedish welfare state was produced by Andrew Brown with a book entitled *Fishing in Utopia: Sweden and the Future that Disappeared* (2008).[2] The narrative is somewhat depressing reading for a Swede. Brown lived in Sweden from the 1970s until the mid-1980s. Twenty years later he revisited Sweden and, in a series of highly personal anecdotes, he illustrated his conclusion that the Sweden he fell in love with no longer exists. In his view, Sweden has lost its unique character. Since the economic and political crisis of the 1990s, he claims, Sweden has become just one of numerous European countries facing problems such as social distinctions and xenophobia. In spite of the fact that Brown's book is autobiographical and is motivated by the author's love of the country rather than being a stringent analysis, it gives us a memorable portrayal of a visionary 'model' country that has fallen on hard times and is no longer exceptional.

While the welfare state had long been considered a precondition of security and a healthy economy, towards the end of the twentieth century it came to be considered a problem. The need for a powerful state in creating welfare was questioned and concepts like the popular welfare state, the Swedish model and the planned society came under attack. Besides the fact that welfare policy was considered as economically inefficient and an ideological mistake, the collectivist and paternalistic nature of the Swedish model society were also challenged. Society's backyard and its 'murky' aspects were illuminated, including society's control of the individual and there was general contempt for human frailty. Leading scholars described the Swedish welfare state as a threat to the citizen's freedom and pointed out how the limbs of the welfare state penetrated far into a person's private sphere.[3]

Criticism of Sweden's welfare arrangements came not only from the right wing but could be heard in social-democrat circles too, in spite of the fact that it was the social democrats who originally introduced the policy.[4] The struggle between defenders and critics can be partially seen as a conflict about the Swedish identity as well as a fight about history. It was claimed that the success story of Sweden being transformed into a welfare state in the course of only a few decades was idealized and sanitized. That the narrative left out a great deal and was thoroughly tied up in the social democrats' own history in which the begetters and managers of the welfare state are the heroes.[5]

Fundamental changes to Sweden's economy took place during the 1990s. In September 1992 the Swedish *krona* fell dramatically and interest rates momentarily soared to an implausible 500 per cent. The ensuing economic crisis had serious consequences for Sweden and there was a general desire to reform the Swedish model. Important aspects of the welfare state that had been constructed in Sweden since the end of World War II were abandoned and dismantling Sweden's welfare system became something of a mantra. The banks were deregulated, for example, as were capital and labor markets. Concepts like central control and regulation were exchanged for freedom of choice and individual solutions. Having formerly been subject to extreme controls, the Swedish housing provision became one of the most market-controlled in Europe. The idea of a dwelling as a social right was exchanged for the notion of a home being a private investment and a marketable commodity.[6]

Today people regularly speak of the Swedish welfare model as though it remains as it once was. But today's welfare policy differs greatly from that of earlier decades. Nowadays it is the market that is expected to solve problems in the nation's finances. The social democrats are no longer the natural rulers and, while formerly Sweden was ethnically fairly homogeneous, it has now become a multi-cultural society. Some people see this transformation as providing greater freedom from a repressive government and the dynamics of the free market, while others see growing social distinctions and segregation.[7]

The concept of the Nordic model has been much used during the present decade. The term comprises a number of key values like tolerance, justice and equality, and it is not unreasonable to see it as a sort of relaunch of the Swedish model. The term has been emphasized by various political parties but, since 2011, has become a feature of the social democrats' political marketing and the party has registered it as a trademark. This indicates just how powerful the symbolism of this concept actually is.[8]

Beyond the blond

Towards the end of the 1990s and the beginning of the new century the image of Swedish design also changed.[9] Was it really as blond, blue-eyed and functionalist as people maintained? Was it purely a matter of simple, practical utensils and appliances? Who had written the narrative and for what purpose? And was it really right to impose notions of style and taste on other people? One contributing factor in raising these questions was that, during the 1990s, traditional notions were again in circulation about what was specifically Swedish and Scandinavian design.

Jasper Morrison's collection 'Some New Items for the Home' received a great deal of critical acclaim when it was launched in 1989. His neo-modernist collection of simple and elegant furniture was seen as a reaction to the colorful postmodernism of the 1980s but was also regarded as the starting point for a renaissance in Scandinavian design. Morrison pointed the way and seems, in retrospect, to have reanimated modernist ideals even in Sweden.[10]

During the following decade the Swedish design scene was dominated by blond simplicity and the image of Swedish design as functional and undecorated was further strengthened. At the 1998 Milan Furniture Fair the exhibition 'Living in Sweden' was shown. This combined music, fashion, design, food and drink. In the same year, as we have noted, the magazine *Wallpaper* published a whole supplement in which Stockholm was portrayed as a design metropolis with designers to be found in every last corner and with unspoiled countryside within easy reach.[11]

The *Wallpaper* supplement featured, in particular, designers working in a modernist tradition and it reiterated established notions about Swedish design. These were repeated, too, in a number of books about Swedish or Scandinavian design. Many products were admired purely on the grounds that they accorded with nationalist stereotypes, expressed in seductive clichés about the customs of these people of the north and what inspired their aesthetic.

The authors of *Scandinavian Design* (2002) maintained that the Finns compensate their taciturn nature by expressing themselves creatively.[12] In *Design Directory Scandinavia* (1999) the design of the Nordic countries was defined under the heading 'Beauty for All:

The Message of Simplicity and the Culture of Materials.'[13] The title of *New Scandinavian Design* (2004) suggests a different direction, but the themes of the book: 'Democracy,' 'Honesty,' 'Poetry,' 'Innovation,' and 'Craft' affirm and characterize Scandinavian design.[14]

That Swedish design found itself in the international limelight in the 1990s can be viewed against a backdrop of a general neo-modernist trend that was particularly strong in Sweden. But the Swedish boom in almost excessively simple forms should not just be seen as part of a trend but should be viewed in relation to another phenomenon. From having been more or less ostracized on account of its association with the 'nanny' state and with government interference, towards the end of the 1990s the notion of a popular welfare state with its ideology and aesthetic became a popular reference point. In politics and popular culture, in film, design and architecture, people began to refer back to the welfare state which became the core of the national narrative as well as being emblematic of what was specifically Swedish. But in these references there was an evident wave of nostalgia. Initially the welfare state represented a vision of the future but, towards the end of the 1990s and the 2000s, it came to be regarded as a lost paradise.[15]

In fact, Swedish neo-modernist design was rather superficial. Unlike the functionalist models the social and political pathos that had previously motivated the plain style was missing. Instead, the focus was on simplicity for the sake of simplicity. In other words, the welfare-state aesthetic became trendy but hollow. The ideological content was drained off and the aesthetic was transformed into a sort of ubiquitous wallpaper that was even used to provide an attractive image of the country. But Swedish society is hardly as homogeneous and blond as it likes to appear and criticism of the plain, unornamented aesthetic grew.

Towards the end of the 1990s, younger designers in particular sought to puncture the mythical notions about Swedish and Scandinavian design. Their work challenged the idealized image and, rather than living up to the traditional aesthetic norms their agenda included ethnicity, class, gender and politics. The discussion was not restricted to designers but also took place in galleries and in the newspapers and was largely centered on taste and power. One important question was the extent to which a more or less hidden taste agenda had prevailed (Plate 16).[16]

The belief that practicality should be the basis of design is a notion that has long survived in the understanding of what good Swedish design really is. Ideals of taste and quality have been subject to discussion in the past, but the emphasis on practicality and usefulness has not only survived but has been extoled and has acted as a sort of semi-official norm.[17] While functional design has represented what is considered true and good, adornment and decoration have often been used to represent something superficial and unnecessary. The postmodernist discourse of the 1980s on semiotics was readily dismissed as a pathetic intellectual trend and never really established itself. Thus the criticism of the 1990s can be seen partially as a delayed debate on postmodernism.[18]

The historical narrative has ended up on the side of the norms and is characterized by a lack of diversity and exaggerated homogeneity.[19] As a rule it is claimed that Swedish design is characterized by functionality and shaped by critics who are involved with society. Modernist designs tend also to be surrounded by an intellectual raster: visions of an aesthetically classless society. Norms and ideals that have not accorded with the Swedish design identity, in other words mass-produced, standardized everyday products for the common man, have thus been marginalized. Surveys of design history tend also to follow a predetermined, one-track pattern: a relatively uncomplicated portrayal which excludes all traces of theories about consumption, class and gender. Instead, they repeat well-known phenomena and data at the same time that they point to their simplicity and practicality as being typical of Swedish design.[20]

That there was formerly a consensus regarding these matters is explained by the fact that Sweden's design sector consists of a closed circle of people, rather narcissistic in character. Sweden being a small country, relatively few people are involved and they tend to rotate among different positions in the design world. Thus the design sector has been influenced by strong bands of loyalty and a mutually similar approach on the part of weighty players like museums, design historians and the professional organization known as the Swedish Society of Crafts and Design (Svensk form).[21] Nowadays it is generally accepted that the Swedish Society of Crafts and Design has had a powerful influence on the design-history narrative with a normative view of design; that is it has favored certain specific ideals and norms.[22]

Histories of Swedish design, whether written for Swedish or international consumption, constantly focus on the activities of the society with constant references to accepted milestones in the organization's history. The history of the Swedish Society of Crafts and Design is somehow seen as synonymous with Swedish design history in general. These 'milestones' in the past, which include specific exhibitions, manifestos and books, have testified to a development towards a specifically Swedish interpretation of international modernism.[23]

In recent years particularly, the closely related concept of 'Scandinavian design' has also been problematized and questioned.[24] The term has been fenced in by stereotypes and has, according to Kjetil Fallan in his book *Scandinavian Alternative Histories* (2012), served as a 'straightjacket of mythologies.'[25] The book manages to avoid almost everything that has traditionally been characterized as Scandinavian design, using instead a much wider focus on the subject by addressing large areas beyond the usual constricted framework.[26]

Fallan's book is part of a movement in the late 1990s and early 2000s to analyze and criticize the concept of Scandinavian design. This criticism was not generally aimed at IKEA as such but was part of a more wide-ranging discussion and a general revision of deeply rooted perceptions. In this context it is interesting that IKEA largely ignored the discussion, defending the traditional view of Swedish design in order to emphasize its specific profile. Just as with IKEA's use of established notions about the Swedish welfare state the framework of reference for design is obsolete. And even though the critical discussions and questionings were not primarily concerned with IKEA, they are relevant to an understanding of the company's rhetoric.

Old wine in new bottles

A third area where a survey of IKEA's own self-image is relevant is the narrative of the firm as original and innovative. IKEA likes to portray itself as a pioneer in several fields. The

IKEA of the narratives is courageous, creative and different with innovatory solutions and ideas. But the question remains: what is actually original and innovative? This is not necessarily always a matter of having new ideas but of identifying and refining existing concepts. Central in this context is IKEA's capacity for picking up and developing ideas, trends and tendencies and its ability to connect with traditions and cultures.

Flat packages or 'knock-down furniture' are part of IKEA's most prominent hallmark. According to the company's own story, as we have noted, the idea came to a member of the staff like a flash of lightning from a clear sky sometime in the 1950s and was then introduced into the operation. This may be how 'ready-to-assemble' furniture was adopted by IKEA. The table that the IKEA employee unscrewed the legs from so that it would fit in the boot of his car was not, in point of fact, the first knock-down product to be included in the company's range. And furniture of this sort was available from several other sources.[27]

Back in the 1930s, Jean Prouvé produced a series of standard items of furniture that could readily be unscrewed and dispatched in parcel form. His chairs and tables were sold to public institutions like schools and hospitals.[28] In the 1940s there were Swedish designers working with the same ideas and methods as the French architect. The idea behind the Stockholm department store NK with its 'Triva-Bygg' system was to let customers construct furniture themselves with the help of printed instructions and a screwdriver.[29] Writing at the time of the launch, one Swedish journalist opined: 'It is by no means an exaggeration to claim that this series of furniture will revolutionize Swedish furniture production.'[30]

The journalist was right. But it was IKEA who developed the concept. Erik Wørts, who had worked with the 'Triva-Bygg' project, joined IKEA in 1958 where he continued to work on ready-to-assemble furniture.[31] Contrasting with IKEA's official story Ingvar Kamprad has conceded that IKEA was not the first to adopt this technique but borrowed it from elsewhere: 'NK in Stockholm already had a series of so-called knock-down furniture. But they had no idea as to what commercial dynamite they were sitting on. IKEA was able — thanks to the dialogue that I later had with innovative designers — to become the first company to develop the idea programmatically in a business-like manner.'[32]

True or not, Kamprad's explanation confirms IKEA's readiness to refine a good idea. That NK was not a mail-order company helps to explain why it was not more successful in marketing its knock-down furniture; something much more suited to a mail-order firm than a traditional department store.[33] Also, NK had traditionally aimed at a more affluent clientele. It was from NK, too, that IKEA borrowed the idea of presenting furniture in inspirational stagings with underlying educational ambitions. Lennart Ekmark, who introduced and was responsible for presentation in the IKEA stores for many years, realized that this mode of presentation was not just commercially successful but he also shared the educational ideas. That the settings in the stores could provide guidance to customers with carefully worked furnishing proposals.[34]

But NK was not the first company to use this technique of not just presenting single products but complete room settings. In the latter half of the nineteenth century, settings began to be shown in the new department stores which distinguished them from the usual sorts of smaller retail shops. The sales strategy was focused on creating a total effect with the right atmosphere. In these contexts it was often a matter of magnificent, theatrical stagings in which the products might seem to be unimportant details in a larger whole. The presentations were luxurious and, at times, exotic.[35]

The yellow and blue IKEA bags that are so associated with IKEA and that are piled up at the entrance to the store are yet another example of a concrete concept that the company has snapped up and developed. In this case the idea was taken from the Carrefour chain of shops.[36] The playroom full of colorful plastic balls designed to entertain children while their parents shop has also come to be associated with IKEA (Figure 5.1). The idea was launched by Charlotte Rude and Hjördis Olson-Une, who were inspired by similar rooms in Denmark.[37]

Several of the ideas and sales strategies that are now emblematic of IKEA were, thus, not new. What was creative and innovative was being able to snap up and develop the ideas and, not least, the ability to adapt the IKEA narrative so that the company appeared to be innovative. Here lies an important reason for the company's success. IKEA has not only developed other people's ideas but has also refined certain established traditions. It is particularly interesting to compare IKEA with the Swedish Cooperative Movement (KF), which enjoyed a huge influence on Swedish life in the decades immediately prior to and after World War II. Lasse Brunnström even claims that: 'Without serious exaggeration one may claim that between the 1930s and the 1970s, KF was involved in the average Swede's life from cradle to grave.'[38]

Figure 5.1 Children's playroom, 1980s. (Used with the permission of Inter IKEA Systems B.V. © Inter IKEA Systems B.V.)

KF was founded in 1899 with the aim of lowering food prices for ordinary people and lessening their dependence on private tradesmen. It soon grew into a gigantic organization, in formal terms politically independent but frequently associated with the ideals of the labor movement. Inspired by US retail chains, KF pioneered 'self-service stores' in Sweden using standardized and functional fittings in the shops. As early as 1924 KF established its own architectural office which came to have a huge influence on architectural expression in Sweden in the twentieth century. The office's plain, rational, matter-of-fact modernism reached into every corner of Sweden and influenced the greater part of what was built in Sweden immediately prior to and after the war: thousands of food shops, department stores, theaters, town halls, schools, restaurants, dwellings and factory premises.[39]

Similarity was a central aspect of the KF brand. The operations took place within a defined, ideological framework with the express ambition of commissioning long series of products and of developing appropriate norms. The architectural office had an almost stifling system of rules governing how bathrooms, halls, bedrooms and sitting rooms should be set out. In addition to this, KF also produced basic ranges of clothes, furniture and food products.[40] Educational strategies and information campaigns were also an early focus. KF became emblematic of what Peder Aléx has described as rational consumption, which was a matter of educating consumers in self-control, thrift, common sense and carefully planned purchases. But, in consumer terms, what is right and wrong? KF lauded whatever was standardized, functional and practical in daily use.[41]

Establishing direct links between KF and IKEA is problematic but there is no doubt that KF provided a culture and a tradition to build on. And it may well seem reasonable to compare IKEA's dominance, at least in the Swedish market with a combination of budget prices and a positively charged brand, with the role that KF played in the Swedish welfare state when at its peak.[42] This is not a matter of similarities with specific KF programs, but the way in which IKEA redirected an existing tradition and culture. IKEA linked up with a tradition of popular education as to taste. The path had already been prepared, but IKEA was there at the right time and in the right place.

In Sweden, the economically successful decades between the end of World War II and the oil crisis in 1973–4 are known as the record years. Constant economic growth made social reforms possible and also led to a large increase in people's standard of living. All the indicators pointed upwards. In 1964 the social-democrat government announced that a million new housing units were to be built in the ensuing ten-year period and the next year the program got underway.[43] Each of the new dwellings naturally needed furniture and household utensils, and between 1950 and 1975 the purchasing power of the Swedish populace doubled. Higher incomes and the attendant higher levels of consumption made it possible for people to furnish their homes in their own way with what was available in the shops.[44]

Enthusiasm for home furnishing in Sweden cannot be understood merely in terms of educational programs or propaganda about the importance of interior design. Building the one million units of housing proceeded apace and the populace had more money for buying furniture and suchlike. One should see IKEA's growth in this light. The company's expansion was aided by Sweden's economic success and by the need to furnish the increasing numbers of new apartments.

IKEA in the limelight

In more recent decades IKEA has found itself in the line of fire from critics and has been closely monitored. Moral considerations have been paramount, but also Kamprad's own history. In 1994 it was revealed that, during most of his youth, Kamprad had been active in movements and groups with Nazi undertones. These revelations caused a great stir in the media, shaking not only Kamprad but also IKEA.

Kamprad comes from a Sudeten German family and his links with Germany remained strong following Hitler's rise to power as well as throughout the war. The picture of his political and ideological commitment has been added to and intensified over the years. He took his first contacts with Nazism in 1942 and he continued to be active in such circles at least until 1950. According to Elisabeth Åsbrink the Swedish security police opened a file on Kamprad in 1943, under the heading 'Nazi.' He sympathized with the fascist New Swedish Movement (Nysvenska Rörelsen) for a number of years after the end of World War II and was on friendly terms with the movement's leader Per Engdahl. As late as 2010 he claimed in an interview that Engdahl 'was a great man, a view I shall maintain as long as I live.'[45]

The crisis management undertaken by IKEA after the 1994 revelation is a rhetorical masterpiece. Kamprad apologized with striking humility and, over the years, the apologies have been repeated.[46] In a letter to IKEA's staff in conjunction with the original revelations he wrote: 'You have been young yourselves and perhaps there is something in your youth that now, long afterwards you think was rather stupid. In that case you will understand me better. And add to that the fact that it was 40 or 50 years ago. Now, in retrospect, I know that I forgot to mention this among my fiascos at an early stage, but that is now spilled milk.'[47]

After the 1994 revelation, Kamprad commissioned journalist Bertil Torekull to write a book about him and IKEA. This might be regarded as an attempt at repairing the damage that his political history had caused. Torekull describes Kamprad's Nazi contacts, but these are regarded as mere youthful aberrations. He also gives an account of the dramatic days when the information was made public, portraying a very brave man. Just as in the creation narrative of IKEA, Kamprad is described as a pugnacious underdog: 'He drank some coffee left over from last Friday's coffee break and he found two rather dry buns and that was all he ate during two days of hard work.'[48] His fighting spirit and his perseverance cause Kamprad to appear in a positive light and as a survivor.

Kamprad's Nazi past gave rise to much discussion in Sweden and people drew parallels between IKEA's founder and the popular welfare state on the one side and Hitler and the Third Reich on the other. In a series of articles Kamprad was portrayed as a species of postmodern or global Hitler who had tried to create something even bigger than the Third Reich. Added to this was a picture of IKEA's combination of traditional community and modernity, exaggerated 'Swedishness' and economic efficiency combined with German national socialism.[49]

It was not just Kamprad's involvement in Nazi movements that gained attention but there have also been attempts to deflate the myths surrounding him on numerous other grounds. He did not, for example, grow up in particularly deprived circumstances nor did he come from such a humble background. True, in the IKEA creation narrative it is not actually claimed that Kamprad came from a poor home but just such an image is communicated, not least thanks to the wider media.

Ingvar Kamprad had become a 'journalists' man' who did not hide his weaknesses but rather, flaunted them, way back in the 1960s. He was classed as a 'farmer's boy' at an early stage and was portrayed in the newspapers as a man who had displayed an extraordinary ability to climb the social ladder. The newspapers liked to emphasize the fact that Kamprad had neither a large country house nor stables full of horses and that his sole pleasure in life consisted of fishing from the riverbank with a rod. This was an image that suited the media perfectly.[50]

In point of fact, Kamprad's family was not at all badly off. His grandfather, Achim Kamprad, had grown up in a German *Schloß* and was related to Paul von Hindenburg who led the German forces in World War I and who later became president of Germany, taking part in the process that led to Adolf Hitler becoming *Reichskanzler*. Achim settled in Sweden in 1896, and the farm where Ingvar Kamprad grew up was much the largest in the district. His mother's side of the family was also quite prosperous, owning a large shop in Älmhult.[51]

A central theme of both IKEA's and Kamprad's own narratives is that he has not actually become rich as an entrepreneur but that he donated his empire to a foreign foundation as early as 1982. According to the company he has worked hard to create an ownership structure that will guarantee independence and long-term survival: 'This is why, since 1982, the IKEA Group has been owned by a foundation in the Netherlands. The foundation is called Stichting INGKA Foundation. Its purpose is to fund charity through the Stichting IKEA Foundation in the Netherlands and to reinvest in the IKEA Group.'[52]

In 2011 new information about the ownership structure was revealed. An investigative television report claimed that the founder had in no way given up his control of the company but had maintained it for decades through a secret foundation, the Interogo Foundation in Liechtenstein. Much of the profits and turnover of the stores had been channeled to this foundation. The conclusion drawn was that the structure was a massive tax-avoidance scheme.[53]

Kamprad maintained that the aim of the foundation was to secure the company's survival and that the assets in question were intended to meet possible financial difficulties and for 'philanthropic purposes': 'Interogo Foundation is controlled by my family and is managed by a board that consists of external members.'[54] Two years later there were further spectacular revelations about ownership strategies.[55]

That large corporations are involved in advanced tax-avoidance schemes resulting in complex ownership and management structures is nothing new or particularly surprising. That the tone was accusatory in respect of IKEA was due to the fact that the company had, over the years, presented itself as a credulous family business and had given the impression that Kamprad had more or less surrendered the company to an independent foundation. The secrecy surrounding all these issues has also opened IKEA up to speculation.

Another area in which IKEA has drawn criticism pertains to the working conditions in companies manufacturing items for IKEA. A television documentary about IKEA's suppliers raised questions about who really paid the bill (that is, who paid for the budget prices in IKEA's stores). The program showed that IKEA used child labor as well as reporting on other unacceptable working conditions.[56]

In 2009 it was revealed that pillows and duvets were filled with feathers plucked from living birds. Down is classed in four categories, the cheapest of which consists of feathers plucked from living birds. This down is cheaper because the birds can be plucked several times before being slaughtered.[57] The Chinese suppliers' action is not illegal as such but is ethically indefensible. We do not know whether IKEA was aware of the circumstances but the company has a reputation for putting pressure on suppliers to reduce prices.

Three years later an IKEA subsidiary was accused of felling a large tract of virgin forest in Russian Karelia. The company had permission from the international forestry organization Forest Stewardship Council (FSC), whose task it is to protect unique forests. That organization has received large sums of money from IKEA which has given rise to talk about corrupt practices.[58] In the same year it was confirmed that political prisoners in the German Democratic Republic had manufactured parts for IKEA's furniture from the 1960s until the 1980s.[59] IKEA had no direct contact with the supplier but, in the succeeding debate, critics asked why the company had let itself be satisfied by empty assurances about acceptable working conditions and carefully controlled inspections of the factories.[60]

Criticism of IKEA is not restricted to ethics and to matters relating to manufacturing. The company has also been criticized for adapting, in the manner of a chameleon, to current political and cultural contexts that conflict with IKEA's general narrative of gender equality. In 2012 it was revealed that the company's Saudi Arabian catalog departed fundamentally from other IKEA catalogs in that in certain illustrations, women and girls had been removed by retouching (Plate 17). In other catalogs, four designers responsible for collections were presented. In the Saudi catalog the four designers had been reduced to three, the female designer having been removed.[61]

IKEA points to the fact that it has contributed to social change through the cheapness of its products. Kamprad has even claimed: 'To put it rather grandly, our business philosophy *de facto* contributes to a process of democratization.'[62] But are budget prices always a good thing? And where exactly does the ethical boundary lie in the effort to reduce costs? IKEA's constantly repeated motto and its overall vision is: 'A better everyday life.' The question is whether IKEA has actually improved the quality of everyday life for everyone, that is to say, whether constantly seeking to achieve lower prices necessarily leads to exploitation.

The socially responsible corporation

IKEA's slogan 'Low Price. But Not at Any Price,' signaling social consciousness and responsibility, should not be seen as mere rhetoric or as a defensive comeback. IKEA has embraced the criticism by improving its policies and control of manufacturers. But the company can also be said to have made use of the criticism in building its brand. IKEA's stores are often presented as the good example: the company with a social commitment that seeks to do what is right with regard to ethical, social and environmental issues.[63] In other words, it is very possible that IKEA actually does behave more honorably than other multinational corporations.

In IKEA's history, as presented on the firm's website, earlier decades from the 1950s onwards are concerned with when and where new stores were opened as well as details of special collections and products. But in the twenty-first century IKEA appears to be more like a philanthropic organization than a company dealing in furniture. Central to the narrative of the most recent decade is the collaboration with socially credible organizations such as Save the Children, UNICEF (United Nations Children's Fund) and WWF (World Wide Fund for Nature). There is no mention of new stores or products but there is information about IKEA's extreme demands with regard to acceptable working conditions to be observed by suppliers, regulations regarding emissions in air and water and, not least, how IKEA seeks to prevent child labor.[64]

Environmental and ethical matters are also the theme of a book by former IKEA CEO Anders Dahlvig entitled *The IKEA Edge: Building Global Growth and Social Good at the World's Most Iconic Home Store* (2011) in which IKEA is presented as a model business. The aim of the argument is to try to establish what is required for reaching traditional business goals such as profits and increased turnover while, at the same time, contributing to a better society in the widest sense.[65]

Both Kamprad himself and IKEA have shown unique powers of resistance against negative criticism. In 2001 *Newsweek* employed the metaphor 'The Teflon Multinational,' claiming that criticism fails to adhere to the company and, in this connection, noted IKEA's collaboration with Greenpeace.[66] That accusations run off IKEA like water off a duck's back may be due to the company actually being infused by a social and ethical consciousness. But the Teflon strategy has also been reproached for just being a façade. Former staffer Johan Stenebo claims that IKEA does not consciously contravene environmental regulations, but he questions the purpose of the virtuous collaborations. According to Stenebo the company allies itself with trusted organizations in order to gain their loyalty; that is to say, in order to use them as a sort of alibi or hostage. Critics thus regard the strategy as calculating and cynical.[67]

That companies collaborate with aid organizations or donate money to them is nothing unusual. One unique example though is Adriano Olivetti who, like Kamprad, has been called a moral capitalist. Back in the 1950s his employees enjoyed free health care while new mothers could stay at home for several months on full play. The company also built housing for its workers; which is by no means unique. But to commission famous architects to design simple dwellings, as Olivetti did, was certainly unusual. Equally unusual was the company's support for culture. Olivetti started literary and philosophical journals and organized lectures on art and science during the lunch breaks.[68]

During the current century the notion of corporate social responsibility has become accepted. It is partly a matter of advertising and partly of taking up public positions. One aim is, of course, to make a contribution to the good of society in general rather than merely seeking to maximize profit. But it is also a question of image. Companies are no longer judged purely by prices and by the quality of their products, but their commitment to society can cause them to appear to be sympathetic and loyal and these qualities can then be used for marketing purposes.[69]

IKEA does not just highlight its collaboration with environmental organizations but has also used well-known public figures in the field to endorse the company. In a book entitled *Democratic Design* (1995) Victor Papanek, best known for his commitment to environmental matters and his advocacy of socially and ecologically responsible design of products, tools, and community infrastructures, wrote: 'One thing is certain: IKEA will continue in the forefront—ecologically, socially and culturally—of making things that work, possess beauty and are affordable.'[70]

Notes

1   Jenny Andersson and Kjell Östberg, *Sveriges historia 1965–2012* (Stockholm: Norstedts, 2013), pp. 14–21. See also Urban Lundberg and Mattias Tydén, 'In Search of the Swedish Model. Contested Historiography,' in Helena Mattsson and Sven-Olof Wallenstein (eds), *Swedish Modernism. Architecture, Consumption and the Welfare State* (London: Black Dog, 2010), pp. 36–49; Jenny Andersson and Mary Hilson, 'Images of Sweden and the Nordic Countries,' *Scandinavian Journal of History*, Vol. 34, No. 3 (2009), pp. 219–28.

2   Andrew Brown, *Fishing in Utopia*, 2008 (London: Granta, 2008).

3   An important contribution and a sort of starting point for a re-evaluation of the history of the Swedish model can be found in Yvonne Hirdman, *Att lägga livet tillrätta. Studier i svensk folkhemspolitik* (Stockholm: Carlsson, 1989). For a survey of historical writing on Swedish welfare policy see Urban Lundberg and Mattias Tydén, 'Stat och individ i svensk välfärdspolitisk historieskrivning,' *Arbejderhistoria*, No. 2 (2008); Lundberg and Tydén, 'In Search of the Swedish Model. Contested Historiography' in Mattsson and Wallenstein 2010.

4   The inquiry into political power in Sweden was a government study and a social-science research project ordered by Deputy Prime Minister Ingvar Carlsson in 1985. The final report was issued in 1990: *Demokrati och makt i Sverige*, Stockholm: Allmänna förlaget, Statens offentliga utredningar, SOU, 1990:44.

5   Andersson and Östberg 2013, p. 379. A study that discusses how Swedish Social Democracy has portrayed its own and Sweden's history from a historiographical perspective is Åsa Lindeborg, *Socialdemokraterna skriver historia. Historieskrivning som ideologisk maktresurs 1892–2000*, Diss. (Stockholm: Atlas, 2001).

6   Andersson and Östberg 2013, pp. 358, 366, 408–12.

7   Andersson and Östberg 2013, pp. 16–20.

8   On the political struggle concerning the terminology see Per Svensson, 'Striden om historien. Historieätarna,' *Magasinet Arena*, No. 1 (2013), pp. 40–8.

9   As early as the 1960s there was discussion of the dominant approach and the norms of taste in Swedish design but there was renewed focus in the 1990s. On the discussions in the 1960s see Cilla Robach, *Formens frigörelse. Konsthantverk och design under debatt i 1960-talets Sverige*, Diss. (Stockholm: Arvinius, 2010).

10 An early and central example of 1990s Swedish modernism is the collection Element (1991) which consisted of artifacts by a number of designers including Björn Kussofsky, Thomas Sandell, Pia Wallén and Tom Hedqvist. The basic characteristic of the series was a conscious accolade to the austere design of the 1940s and 1950s. Several of the designers later played a prominent role in IKEA's PS collection. Hedvig Hedqvist, *1900–2002. Svensk form. Internationell design* (Stockholm: Bokförlaget DN, 2002), pp. 206–7.

11 *Wallpaper*, Design guide Stockholm, No. 11 (1998).

12 The authors also claim that the Finns have an innate respect for material and an almost mythical affinity with nature. Charlotte and Peter Fiell, *Scandinavian Design* (Köln: Taschen, 2002), pp. 34, 36.

13 Bernd Polster (ed.), *Designdirectory Scandinavia* (London: Pavilion, 1999), p. 9.

14 Katherine E. Nelson, *New Scandinavian Design* (San Francisco: Chronicle Books, 2004).

15 Jenny Andersson, 'Nordic Nostalgia and Nordic Light. The Swedish model as Utopia 1930–2007,' *Scandinavian Journal of History*, Vol. 34, No. 3 (2009), pp. 229–45.

16 There were numerous exhibitions focusing on such issues as taste, gender and class, among them: 'Stiligt, fiffigt, blont' (Galleri Y1 1997), 'Formbart' (Liljevachs konsthall 2005), 'Invisible Wealth' (Färgfabriken 2003), 'Konceptdesign' (Nationalmuseum 2005), as well as a succession of exhibitions at the Agata gallery. The matter has also been discussed in books including: Love Jönsson (ed.), *Craft in Dialogue. Six Views On a Practice in Change* (Stockholm: IASPIS, 2005); Zandra Ahl and Emma Olsson, *Svensk smak. Myter om den moderna formen* (Stockholm: Ordfront, 2001); Sara Kristoffersson, *Memphis och den italienska antidesignrörelsen*, Diss. (Göteborg: Acta Universitatis Gothoburgensis, 2003); Cilla Robach (ed.), *Konceptdesign* (Stockholm: Nationalmuseum, 2005); Brunnström 2010. A foreign example in which the conflict between Swedish neo-modernism and the youthful antimodernist generation found expression was the exhibition 'Beauty and the Beast' (Crafts Council Gallery, London 2004) curated by Lesley Jackson.

17 Brunnström 2010, pp. 366–7.

18 Sara Kristoffersson, 'Svensk form och IKEA' in Andersson and Östberg 2013, pp. 108–13; Sara Kristoffersson, 'Swedish Design History,' *Journal of Design History*, Vol. 24, Issue 2 (2011), pp. 197–9.

19 Brunnström 2010, pp. 16–17.

20 Brunnström 2010, pp. 16–17; Sara Kristoffersson, 'Designlandet Sverige fattigt på forskning,' *Svenska Dagbladet*, November 3, 2010.

21 Sara Kristoffersson and Christina Zetterlund, 'A Historiography of Scandinavian Design' in Kjetil Fallan (ed.), *Scandinavian Design. Alternative Histories* (Oxford: Berg, 2012).

22 Sara Kristoffersson and Christina Zetterlund, 'A Historiography of Scandinavian Design' in Kjetil Fallan (ed.), *Scandinavian Design. Alternative Histories* (Oxford: Berg, 2012); Brunnström 2010, p. 16.

23 An illustrative example is the book *Formens rörelse. Svensk form genom 150 år* (1995) with a title as ambiguous as it is doubtful. There is an underlying intention not just to portray the history of the Swedish Society of Crafts and Design, but also to provide a survey of the history of Swedish design: how form is expressed and how it changes and why. The book implies that the history of Swedish design is identical to the society's history. See Kristoffersson and Zetterlund in Fallan 2012. There are numerous examples of books that follow the society's own description of its history very closely, for example Susanne Helgesson and Kent Nyberg, *Svenska former* (Stockholm: Prisma, 2000).

24 Criticizing and questioning the concept of Scandinavian design is nothing new. Back in the 1950s and 1960s, in parallel with the victorious progress of Scandinavian design throughout the world, there was a critical debate in Sweden. Evaluations were questioned and norms were broken. This relatively little known occurrence is addressed in Robach 2010.

25 K. Fallan (ed.), *Scandinavian Design. Alternative Histories* (Oxford: Berg, 2012), p. 1.

26 Fallan (2012) distinguishes himself from Halén and Wickman (2003). Their title *Scandinavian Design Beyond the Myth* sounds promising but the book almost totally neglects contemporary design and crafts that have been concerned with penetrating the myths surrounding

Scandinavian design. In the section devoted to contemporary Scandinavian design they focus almost entirely on items that live up to the traditional image.

27 IKEAs first knock-down furniture was presented in the 1953 catalog. Among the products was the 'Max' table.

28 Atelier Jean Prouvé was started in 1931 and, during the 1930s, Prouvé also started producing metal elements including façades and doors intended for mounting on site. On Prouvé's furniture see Catherine Coley, 'Furniture: Design, Manufacture, Marketing' in Alexander von Vegesack (ed.), *Jean Prouvé. The Poetics of the Technical Object* (Weil am Rhein: Vitra Design Stiftung, 2006), pp. 314–29.

29 The series was created in connection with a furniture competition in 1943. First prize was awarded to 'Ta I trä' [Touch wood] designed by Elias Svedberg with assistance from Erik Wörts and Lena Larsson. The proposal was realized and it marked a turning point in the history of Swedish furniture. The series was called 'Triva-bygg' and it was launched via the NK department store. Over the years items were added and the series consisted of cupboard units, dining table and chairs. Monica Boman, 'Vardagens decennium' in Boman 1991, pp. 244–8.

30 Gotthard Johansson, 'Den verkliga standardmöbeln,' *Svenska Dagbladet*, July 14, 1944.

31 Atle Bjarnestam 2009, p. 41; Wickman 1995, p. 163.

32 Torekull 2008, p. 79.

33 Wickman, 'A Furniture Store for Everyone' in Bengtsson 2009. Unpaginated catalog.

34 Interview with Lennart Ekmark 2009. The educational ambitions were also noted in Atle Bjarnestam 2009, p. 208; Wickman in Bengtsson 2009.

35 Orsi Husz, *Drömmars värde. Varuhus och lotteri i svensk konsumtionskultur 1897–1939*, Diss. (Hedemora: Gidlund, 2004), p. 69.

36 Interview with Lennart Ekmark 2011. The exhibition 'IKEA Explore' at Inter IKEA Culture Center, Älmhult, gives a different explanation. As previously noted, there is a large number of different postcards at the exhibition containing various challenges and problems as well as the IKEA way of solving them—'Challenge' and 'Solution.' Card no. 26 gives an account of the origins of the IKEA bag. An anecdote explains that customers lacked something to put their purchases in and the solution turned out to be: 'On a supplier visit in Taiwan different solutions for a shopping bag were evaluated. To check the strength of a prototype they lifted a woman in the bag! The yellow IKEA shopping bag was born. It was a real innovation for our way of retailing.' Challenge/Solution, Postcard, Inter IKEA Systems, B.V., 2010 (IHA).

37 Wickman, 'A Furniture Store for Everyone' in Bengtsson 2009. In the same publication Bengtsson claims that the idea came from the UK and not from Denmark. Unpaginated catalog.

38 Brunnström 2010, p. 143.

39 Lisa Brunnström, *Det svenska folkhemsbygget. Om Kooperativa förbundets arkitektkontor* (Stockholm: Arkitektur, 2004).

40 During the 1970s the cooperative movement (KF) 1970 presented a series of basic furniture. The intention was that the designs should be anonymous and that the products should function as low-price alternatives to the commercialized furniture market. In 1972 a collection of basic clothing for women was launched and, in 1979 KF launched a range of so-called unbranded convenience goods. On KF's range of basics see Monica Boman, 'Den kluvna marknaden' in Boman 1991, pp. 429–31; Hedqvist 2002, pp. 141–64; Sven Thiberg, 'Dags att undvara. 1970-talet: Insikt om de ändliga resurserna' in Wickman 1995, pp. 268, 271, 278.

41 Peder Aléx, *Den rationella konsumenten. KF som folkuppfostrare 1899–1939* (Stockholm: B. Östlings bokförlag. Symposion, 1994); Helena Mattsson, 'Designing the 'Consumer in Infinity': The Swedish Cooperative Union's New Consumer Policy, c.1970' in Fallan 2012, pp. 65–82.

42 This is also noted in Ola Andersson, 'Folkhemsbygget i KF:s regi,' *Svenska Dagbladet*, June 11, 2004.

43 There are several books about the mass public housing program known as Miljonprogrammet and its positive and negative aspects. See, for example, Karl Olov Arnstberg, *Miljonprogrammet* (Stockholm: Carlsson Bokförlag, 2000).

44 Ehn, Frykgren and Löfgren 1993, pp. 61–2.

45 Kamprad interviewed and quoted in Elisabet Åsbrink, *Och i Wienerwald står träden kvar* (Stockholm: Natur & Kultur, 2012), p. 316; Åsbrink interviewed and quoted in Gustav Sjöholm, 'Fördjupar bilden av Kamprads engagemang,' *Svenska Dagbladet*, August 24, 2011.

46 One example is journalist K-G Bergström's interview with Kamprad on Swedish Television transmitted on October 28, 2008.

47 Kamprad's letter to the staff was headed 'Mitt största fiasko' [My biggest fiasco] (IHA). Parts of the letter and comments on it see Torekull 2008, p. 197.

48 Torekull 2008, p. 195.

49 The newspaper *Dagens Nyheter* published four articles: Henrik Berggren, 'Ideologin som gick hem'; Ingela Lind, 'Kamprad formar en ny världsmedelklass'; Daniel Birnbaum, 'Läran lyder: Billy'; Mikael Löfgren, 'IKEA über alles,' *Dagens Nyheter*, August 30, 1998.

50 Sjöberg 1998, pp. 220–30.

51 Sjöberg 1998; Torekull 2008, pp. 19–23.

52 http://www.IKEA.com/ms/en_GB/about_IKEA/facts_and_figures/about_IKEA_group/index.html (accessed May 28, 2013).

53 *Uppdrag granskning. Made in Sweden—IKEA*, Producer Nils Hansson, Produced by SVT, 2011.

54 Kamprad confirmed the existence of the foundation in an email to the Swedish news agency TT. The email was quoted in a large number of Swedish newspapers in terms such as 'Kamprad acknowledges the existence of a foundation abroad,' *Svenska Dagbladet*, January 26, 2011.

55 Stellan Björk, Lennart Dahlgren and Carl von Schulzenheim, *IKEA mot framtiden*, Stockholm: Norstedts, 2013.

56 *Två världsföretag. Tomtens verkstad—IKEAs bakgård.* Producent Andreas Franzén, sänt på Sveriges Television, December 22, 1997.

57 'IKEA lovade för mycket om dunet,' *Aftonbladet*, February 8, 2009; Stenebo 2009, pp. 189–90.

58 *Uppdrag granskning*, Sveriges Television.

59 The information was presented in 2011 in a German TV program and was then relayed by Swedish Television. IKEA commissioned accountants Ernst & Young to investigate the information which was confirmed in a report. Ernst & Young went through some 20,000 pages of documentation in IKEA's internal archive and 80,000 documents from German archives. Some ninety people were also interviewed. In the autumn of 2012 there were reports in the press, principally in Swedish and German newspapers. Jan Lewenhagen, 'IKEA bekräftar: Politiska fångar användes i produktionen,' *Dagens Nyheter*, November 16, 2012.

60 Fredrik Persson, 'IKEAs platta försvar av straffarbete,' Aftonbladet, November 21, 2012.

61 The subject was debated in the autumn of 2012. See, for example, Ossi Carp, 'Inga kvinnor i saudisk IKEAkatalog,' Dagens Nyheter, October 1, 2021; Nesrine Malik, 'No women please, we're Saudi Arabian IKEA,' *The Guardian*, October 2, 2012.

62 Kamprad quoted in Torekull 2008, p. 2010. Staffan Bengtsson repeated this, claiming that IKEA 'has exerted more influence over the democratisation process than elected politicians'

(Bengtsson 2009). Unpaginated catalog. The exhibition and the publication were financed by IKEA and are further in Chapter 6.

63 A. Dahlvig, *Med uppdrag att växa. Om ansvarsfullt företagande* (Lund: Studentlitteratur, 2011); Karen Lowry Miller, Adam Piore and Stefan Theil, 'The Teflon Shield,' *Newsweek*, Vol. 137, Issue, 11, March 12, 2001.

64 http://www.IKEA.com/ms/en_GB/about_IKEA/our_responsibility/partnerships/ (accessed October 15, 2013).

65 Dahlvig 2011.

66 Lowry Miller, Piore, Theil 2001.

67 Stenebo 2009, pp. 186–91.

68 One section in Torekull (2008) is called 'Den goda kapitalisten' [The virtuous capitalist], pp. 209–217. Torekull (2011) also applies this epithet to Kamprad, pp. 35–52. On Olivetti's personnel policy see Sibylle Kicherer, *Olivetti. A Study of the Management of Corporate Design*, (London: Trefoil, 1989), pp. 14–15.

69 On the concept of Corporate Social Responsibility see *Harvard Business Review on Corporate Responsibility* (Boston: Harvard Business School, 2003).

70 Victor Papanek, 'IKEA and the Future: A Personal View' in *Democratic Design* (Inter IKEA Systems B.V., 1995), p. 261.

6
DEMOCRACY FOR SALE

'Oh! . . . look at that, Jean,' Denise Baudu excitedly exclaims as she finds herself standing in front of a shop window on the corner of the Rue de la Michodière and the Rue Neuve-Saint-Augustin in Émile Zola's novel *Au Bonheur des Dames* published in 1883.[1] Denise has just met up with the phenomenon that changed the buying habits of the Western world and the way in which we relate to material products: the new department stores.

Research into the consumer culture that developed in the second half of the nineteenth century makes frequent reference to Zola's writings about a fictional department store in Paris offering a range of products that attracted custom and awakened desire. Not only could one shop in the modern department store, but one could also succumb to dreams, looking at the wares, and yearning. Zola's novel, which is both a description of the developing culture of the department store and an interpretation of its role in society, was based on extensive research into French stores which Zola termed *cathédrals de commerce moderne.*[2]

The department store rapidly became, and still remains, a symbol of trade, hedonism and consumer dreams. The store is a place that has its foundations in people's yearnings and desires, a place that promises to fulfill our human fantasies and hopes. In this respect, IKEA's stores are no different from other stores. This is expressed in one of IKEA's numerous slogans: 'Stop Dreaming. Live Today.'[3] The challenge implies that IKEA's stores, thanks to their low prices, can realize our dreams. The low price 'is the magical ingredient which so uncompromisingly divides the indispensable from the attainable.'[4]

Dreams and consumption are connected with each other, if not totally interlinked. 'Sell them dreams,' William Leach cites an expert on decoration, 'Visions of what might happen if only . . . After all, people don't buy things, they buy hope.'[5] IKEA's studied interiors are fairly realistic, but they still arouse people's dreams and the company's stores are definitely part of modern consumer culture. In this final chapter of my book it is natural to want to place the company in just such a context and, thereby, to strengthen the framework in which to interpret it. I intend to summarize the results of the book and thus to bring visibility to aspects of IKEA's success, as well as relating this to our contemporary megatrend: consumerism.

The best story wins

IKEA's extraordinary success naturally appeals to our love of anything 'feel-good.' It is a saga of a heroic past, but it is also a story of development and progress. In the narrative of what IKEA is or seeks to be we can read about a company that has ambitions, an idea and a philosophy. All this is kept alive through being handed down orally and in writing. IKEA nurtures its peculiar identity by portraying itself as being, in some sense, different. The theme is that IKEA is different from other corporations. IKEA has dared to do things differently and, to this end, has developed unconventional methods and new concepts as well as unique sales strategies. The stores have gone their own way: the IKEA way.

In spite of its Swedish profile, the story of how Kamprad created IKEA can be read as a variant on the American dream, a capitalist story based on the idea that anyone can be successful, regardless of his or her social or economic situation. The force and effectiveness of the company's narratives become apparent when one realizes how effectively they function on a global level. Simple fables about success are generally easy to get across. The IKEA narratives live their own lives. They are handed on and repeated for staff, customers and media, appearing at museums, in books and with the Swedish government. The tales and the attendant rhetoric are seldom confronted with reality but are uncritically reproduced.

An example of this is afforded by *IKEA. The Book* (2010), which is an ingratiating story without even marginal question marks. The book portrays Kamprad as a hero and IKEA gets to illustrate Swedish welfare policy and social responsibility.[6] In a succession of wider-ranging surveys of design history, too, IKEA's basic philosophy is claimed to be the task of giving everyone an equal opportunity of being able to furnish a beautiful home regardless of the family's financial situation. And such narratives generally go on to maintain that the company pursues Swedish ideals, norms and visions.[7] Over a long period, the permanent display at Sweden's national design museum—the Röhsska Museum in Gothenburg—was called *From Ellen Key to IKEA*.[8] The title suggests that there is a direct line of development from Ellen Key's social and democratic pathos to the IKEA chain of stores.

Another example is that of the exhibition *IKEA at Liljevalchs* (2009) which was shown in Stockholm's municipal art gallery (Figure 6.1). It normally costs about SEK 600,000 for an institution to produce an exhibition on this scale but, on this occasion, the exhibition was much more expensive. The extra expenditure was paid for by IKEA.[9] The company's success story was presented in a thoroughly educational manner. But the exhibition was also a grand celebration which could equally well have been organized by the company itself. It was claimed that IKEA was not involved in mounting the exhibition.[10]

That the gallery was not interested in 'biting the hand' that was paying the bills, or censoring itself, was evident. Naturally, IKEA was not responsible for designing the exhibition but one must ask whether the gallery more or less consciously adapted itself to the will of the company. Rather than marking a distance and maintaining an independent approach, the exhibition dealt with criticism of IKEA—for example claims of plagiarism—in the politest terms. The revelation that, in his youth, Kamprad had sympathized with a Swedish ultra-nationalist/Nazi/fascist movement was passed over in a couple of lines in the catalog.[11]

Also in 2009, an exhibition entitled *Democratic Design* was held at the Pinakothek der Moderne in Munich. Just as at the exhibition in Stockholm, a selection of the company's products from the 1950s onwards was displayed. The title, *Democratic Design*, came from the company's own arsenal of slogans while also suggesting that IKEA has adopted

Figure 6.1 Exhibition 'IKEA at Liljevalchs,' Liljevalchs Konsthall, Stockholm, 2009. (Used with the permission of Inter IKEA Systems B.V. © Inter IKEA Systems B.V.)

a socially committed design philosophy. A book entitled *Democratic Design: IKEA— Furniture for Mankind* (2009) was produced in conjunction with the exhibition, commissioned by IKEA and authored by Heiner Uber. The book was on sale at the museum and at IKEA stores in Germany.[12]

Many companies pay a great deal of attention to how they relate their past, including such narratives in the brand. Books and exhibitions are part of their marketing strategies and some companies even build museums with a view to preserving their past. IKEA has realized the potential in just such a strategy and is building a museum in Älmhult.[13] But it is particularly effective when the company's history is presented by other people and in a non-commercial context. When these narratives are presented in the media or in books and exhibitions, they gain in legitimacy, credibility and status. A primordial example is the Olivetti exhibition at the Museum of Modern Art (MoMA) in 1952.

There are many reasons for IKEA's success, but it is clear that the narratives are important both within the company and externally. But narratives by themselves do not create forceful marketing strategies as such. And so we must ask what it is that makes IKEA's narratives so convincing and so successful. One important factor is that the narratives are all about success and prosperity. But there are many companies that used just such a concept. Specific to the IKEA narratives is the fact that they also comprise two central themes that are often intertwined and that are constantly repeated: social responsibility and Swedishness.

IKEA links its low prices to social and ideological ambitions. An important aspect of the official history of the firm is the founder's ambition of making a beautiful home accessible to everyone. This philosophy permeates all the firm's operations and IKEA's social responsibility runs like a thread through the corporate mythology. The reason for the pricing policy is, therefore, the vision of creating a better everyday life for a large number of people by making it possible for more people to have beautiful homes. The catalog for the Stockholm exhibition, IKEA at Liljevalchs, ends with a statement by Kamprad that sounds like a manifesto: 'We have an important mission: the many people! They need us.'[14]

The low prices do not seem to be an end in themselves but are motivated by a sort of self-imposed assignment that signals to the world that IKEA is different from other companies that are primarily concerned with profits. Social responsibility and a desire to meet people's basic needs form the motor that drives the operation. The notion of IKEA as an altruistic organization is particularly evident in the creation narrative but is repeated, too, in other contexts. It is also personified by Kamprad himself whose image seems to correspond to and be synchronized with the brand itself.

Numerous more or less improbable and servile stories about Kamprad, his actions, attitudes and character, circulate within IKEA and in the wider world. These stories cover a wide range of issues from his brilliant solutions to corporate problems and his management skills, to his modesty and his frugal lifestyle. The business mantra at IKEA is one of cost-consciousness. It is for the benefit of the customers that all the employees, including the founder and owner of the company, economize.

Even though Kamprad no longer has any formal position in the company he continues to have a symbolic importance and one might speak of the corporate culture in terms of

Kamprad's hegemony. In the foundation narrative the IKEA stores and the founder are one and the same thing. Kamprad's personality lives in symbiosis with that of IKEA. His personal thriftiness has become emblematic of a low-cost company that wastes no resources. No excesses are allowed at IKEA since the company claims that it has a social responsibility.

Kamprad is generally portrayed as honest, personable and humane; a humble and kind-hearted man who wants the best deal for his customers. There are constant portraits along these lines, all of them reiterating much the same stuff using the same clichés. There is, quite simply, a repertoire of standard answers and the image of Kamprad that we receive becomes suddenly impersonal and lacking in nuances. In this perspective Kamprad appears as a brilliant stage director who has claimed for himself a preferential right of interpretation. It is as though Kamprad has written the play and is performing the principal role himself.

The social responsibility and ideological conviction are declaimed in IKEA's own paraphrases of modernistic mottos. Well-known slogans like 'Beauty in the Home' and 'Better Things for Everyday Life' are transformed into catch phrases like 'Design for All' and 'Democratic Design'; a concept that IKEA has almost made its own.[15] At the beginning of the last century there were many who claimed that the answer to the lack of housing and impoverished living conditions lay in rational mass production, which was associated with democracy and social development.

Many of the products that were designed at the Bauhaus, for example, remained as prototypes and were not put into production until years later. They were not immediately mass-produced in the way that their designers had intended.[16] IKEA associates itself with political and social radicalism. The company claims not just to share its visions, but also to realize them. While modernist pioneers dreamed of housing and furnishings being available to all, IKEA has actually put this into practice.

In the last decade IKEA has emphasized its social responsibility by highlighting the company's ethical guidelines, not least in selecting manufacturers. The company has also publicized its collaboration with organizations like the World Wildlife Fund, the Red Cross and UNICEF. Also emphasized are the company's awareness and engagement in issues like diversity and ethnicity. IKEA appears as a company that is remarkably politically correct, sympathetic and socially responsible.

IKEA's self-portrayal as a committed and socially aware organization fits very well with the Swedish emphasis in its marketing. Sweden is presented as a country that is characterized by its progressive values, social-democratic welfare policy and its wide acceptance of modernist design. IKEA, in turn, appears as a modern company that has developed out of Swedish social commitment. The company claims to work with the same values, ideals and principles as Swedish welfare policies, with a focus on solidarity, justice and equality. IKEA and Swedish welfare policy, in this very simplified model, appear to be the same thing.

But the Swedish profile does not only comprise elements that signal social awareness, for IKEA also uses numerous national markers that do not allude to social responsibility. Most prominent, perhaps, is a sort of blue and yellow language, a nationally colored costume: the blue and yellow logotype, the blue and yellow exteriors to the stores, the meatballs and the Nordic-sounding product names. IKEA has also taught its staff to behave in a straightforward manner, showing a sense of equality and modesty, and has defined these qualities as being typically Swedish.

With equal regularity IKEA stresses its origins in the province of Småland. Kamprad's background in Småland has been turned into something of a virtue and the region's supposed characteristics—that people from Småland have to fight hard and make good use of the limited resources of the province in order to scrape together a living—are part of the inhabitants' self-image. IKEA's definitions of Sweden, Swedes and people from Småland often seem reminiscent of language once employed by ethnology at a time when scholars sought to explain a people's various temperaments and innate characters.

In IKEA's narrative of Sweden the nation is portrayed not just as a progressive, modern welfare state but also as a rural idyll on the margins of Europe. Photos of red cottages, snow-covered landscapes, moss-covered rocks in the forest, beautiful lakes, slender birch trees, and idyllic country farms are in frequent use. These are all classical and positively charged national markers which, in an international perspective, seem exotic. The blue and yellow elements as well as the romantic images of nature are, indeed, freed from notions of social responsibility and the basically political role that IKEA claims to have adopted, but they help to tone down the firm's commercial aspects.

IKEA's social and national signals have made an important contribution to the success of the business. The marketing strategies adapt and reword the ideological and political ideals and the national markers in order to sharpen the company profile. The narratives give an impression of social responsibility and of Swedishness, but they should be understood in relation to the consumer society of our own epoch.

Seductive interiors

In Zola's novel *Au Bonheur des Dames* the manager of the department store, Octave Mouret, attempts to capitalize on the irrationality of his customers. He wants them to purchase on impulse, to fall for temptation and to visit departments in the store that they had not intended to visit. He wants to make it difficult for customers to act rationally and he seeks to seduce them into buying things that they simply do not need or that they did not previously realize that they lacked. Mouret wants, quite simply, to force them to succumb.

As early as the commencement of the twentieth century people in advertising realized that appealing to people's common sense was meaningless.[17] One of the most prominent figures in the industry, Edward Bernays, claimed that people do not actually think in any strict sense of the word, but that they are governed by impulses, habits and feelings.[18] The people that he meant were the same sort of people that Bernays' uncle, Sigmund Freud, was interested in: irrational people who were ruled by their impulses. And who later became such an important part of the growing consumer culture.[19]

Some decades later Georges Perec portrayed a young couple, Sylvie and Jérôme, who were obsessed with buying things. In his novel *Les Choses. Une histoire des années soixante* (1965) Perec discusses their insatiable craving for home furnishings which bear no relation to the couple's income.[20] At the same time that Sylvie and Jérôme fantasize about their perfect home their world becomes increasingly empty. The novel perfectly illustrates neo-Marxist theories about commodity fetishism and it became something of a cult in left-wing circles; though it was interpreted rather rigidly at the time.

Perec's story cannot really be regarded as a satire, nor does it totally reject the consumer society. Its message is ambiguous. True, the expensive purchases make the couple unhappy, but they also fill an empty hole, giving consolation and a sense of meaning. The authors detached sociological and ironic descriptions of their desires and fantasies makes them seem stupid. But this does not make their dreams less true or less genuine. Perec's portrayal of consumerism is still relevant and significant. People do not just fantasize about their ideal homes but, thanks to the carefully designed interiors in the furniture stores, we are seduced into purchasing all the more. This is something that has been experienced by most visitors to an IKEA store. Fundamental to our Western market economy is the notion that consumption is not just a matter of filling basic needs. It depends on desires, temptations and yearnings, but it also has to do with creating identity, something that Barbara Kruger, for example, has noted. With her critical paraphrase of Descartes' famous maxim, 'I Shop. Therefore I Am,' she places the consumer and consumer society at the center of identity.[21]

Parallels have been drawn between modern society's increasing commercialization and both rationalization and hedonism. There are numerous explanations as to why we consume and there is a growing theoretical interest in the consumer culture.[22] To put it very simply, we can identify two theoretical perspectives. The mass production of items has made it possible for ever larger groups to consume and this has led to the consumer culture being characterized as a democratization of luxury. 'Shopping' is seen as an active, meaningful and identity-generating act. Selecting and purchasing products has come to be associated with self-realization and creativity, something that is liberating and emancipatory. On the other hand, consumption is interpreted as a form of manipulation and seduction.[23]

The idea of our senses being bewitched is not new. That market forces seek to control people is axiomatic. A classic example is to be found in Theodor Adorno and Max Horkheimer's fierce opposition to mass production in their famous essay on the cultural industry in which they claim that this gives an illusion of freedom of choice but that, in point of fact, it leads to passivity. Viewed from a critical perspective, the capitalist system creates new needs or, rather, pseudo needs. We think that we know what we want but, we are exposed to attempts to seduce us and the real problem is that we want to be seduced. In the view of Adorno and Horkheimer it is a matter of false dreams and the erosion of real cultural values.[24] The question then is whether, and in that case who, can determine what is genuine and what is false, what is culturally and morally valuable.

In the Western world's affluent societies the market has to keep launching novelties which are attractive in themselves without actually supplying some formerly unfulfilled need. The modern consumer culture has also been compared with a diffuse and insatiable longing that depends upon our human capacity to constantly experience a sense of need and desire for new products. The consumer does not actually request the product as such but, rather, the expected sense of satisfaction and delight that the item is charged with. Thus it is not a matter of fulfilling a clearly defined need; rather of feeding a nebulous yearning or a desire to be somebody else. But the point is that the things we buy will never satisfy our hunger since they need constantly to be exchanged and updated. Viewed from this sort of angle, consumption has become a central feature of people's lives or, indeed, one of the aims of existence.[25]

In the rich countries of the world material needs are largely met. But the clothes, furniture and household utensils that people already own do not break down sufficiently often to provide the essential stimulus for consumption. And so the novelty value, the surface, the appearance and the packaging become central competitive elements in the market place. Renewal is essential to stimulating or creating demand. To borrow a concept from Wolfgang Fritz Haug: a seductive surface that needs to be replaced at regular intervals.[26]

Besides the fact that the constant production and consumption of manufactured goods does not correspond to any real need, the capitalist system, viewed critically from a consumer perspective, is said to alienate people. Not just from the goods that we produce and consume, but even from our own experiences, feelings and desires. In what Guy Debord called 'The Society of the Spectacle,' human life has to be communicated through products, and the exchange value of such products is the dominant factor.[27]

The rapid post-war transition from a production society to a consumer society, it can be claimed, turned active citizens into identity-seeking consumers. In such a society, people are defined first and foremost as consumers, who also create their identity through consumption. The ego and the product merge and identity becomes established through choice of products. As Zygmunt Bauman has shown, it is paradoxical that, at the same time that people are freer than ever, they are forced into the role of consumers with imagined or enforced needs.[28]

The conclusion must be that people are not nearly as free as they imagine themselves to be. The consumer society does not just colonize our consciousness but causes us to believe that a consumerist lifestyle is something that we have chosen of our own volition when, in point of fact, it has been transformed into an obligation and a virtue. It merely provides short-term satisfaction through shopping, the hunt for new products, new relationships, new interior design and new identities that turn the wheels of growth at a constantly accelerating rate.[29]

It is self-evident that IKEA's business strategy builds on the consumerist ideology. And so it is not difficult to understand that the firm is regarded as an icon of mass consumption. An instructive example can be found in Chuck Palahniuk's novel *Fight Club* (1996) and in the film of the book released in 1999. The story is about how people get stuck in false expectations that consumption is synonymous with pleasure, identity and self-realization which cuts right into IKEAs shopping culture.[30] The protagonist of the story, called 'IKEA boy,' claims that people he knows: 'used to sit in the bathroom with pornography, now they sit in the bathroom with their IKEA furniture catalog.'[31] Consumption is equated with identity and with creating identity. 'IKEA boy' asks himself: 'I'd flip through catalogs and wonder . . . which dining set defines me as a person?'[32] And when his apartment is blown up he exclaims: 'I loved every stick of furniture. That was my whole life. Everything, the lamps, the chairs, the rugs were me. The dishes in the cabinet were me. The plants were me. The television was me. It was me that blew up.'[33]

That IKEA has come to symbolize the ethics of consumerism is also evident in the art world where a succession of artists have focused on the stores and their products. Some have been positive while others have loudly protested.[34] Several of Clay Ketter's works are exclusively constructed using IKEA items, notably the 'Billy' bookcase. One of his aims is to point to the difference between the company and modernist predecessors. While the Bauhaus pioneers devoted much care to the selection of materials and design IKEA, according to Ketter, focuses on crass accounting and marketing.[35]

Anders Jakobsen has also used IKEA products in his art. By disassembling and breaking the mass-produced items he constructs new and unique objects such as a magnificent light-fitting consisting of numerous kitchen strainers, washing-up brushes and tiny lamps. The work consists of, and depends upon, IKEA's mass-produced artifacts while also representing a subtle critique: 'I turn IKEA's rationality against them. Perhaps one could describe this as hijacked consumption.'[36]

*

IKEA is easy to like. The stores have a large range of cheap household wares that provide carefully thought-out and practical furnishing solutions as well as a sympathetic approach. The company helps us to achieve a home that is better organized and more aesthetically pleasing. It is entirely natural that IKEA has made use of the consumer ideology's classical motive forces such as longing, desire and dreams. As noted, the consumer culture is a fundamental precondition for the existence of the store. The aim is to sell as much as possible and to persuade customers to return to the store in the near future and at intervals thereafter. Visits to IKEA are by no means restricted to purchasing items that fill basic needs.

The problem lies in the fact that IKEA pretends that the operation has very different motives. The company does not present itself as part of the consumer culture but justifies itself with its sense of social responsibility and its good will. The image that is communicated is that the company's agenda is not governed by ulterior, commercial motives. It is naturally impossible to say whether the stated aim of emphasizing a social responsibility and of its mission is entirely pragmatic. But it would be reasonable to suppose that the references in question are of some importance. Less public aspects testify to a gap between an official side and the actual circumstances.

Social responsibility is an essential part of IKEA's public profile, and even internally one finds such rhetoric, though mixed in with this, the internal narratives largely deal with the usual commercial aims. The explicit ambition is that: 'no one should leave the IKEA store empty handed.'[37] And that the store should be: 'A highly efficient, and staffed, sales mechanism.'[38] The idea is that visitors should rapidly be transformed into consumers and should be persuaded to buy as much as possible while they are in the store: 'stimulate visitors to make impulse purchases by bringing to their attention needs that they were unaware of before they entered the store. . . .'[39]

IKEA, from the outside, does not look like a traditional multinational corporation. It has worked hard to present itself as genuinely Swedish and familiar. Time and again Kamprad has claimed that he has not really become rich from the business but has more or less given away the chain of stores to an independent foundation. Later it has become evident that IKEA is subject to a highly advanced system of ownership and management structure. That global companies comprise complex economic structures is by no means unusual. In the case of IKEA the impression has been given that the company differs radically from other multinationals. Against a background of revelations of complex financial constructions the picture of IKEA as a more or less idealistic organization or a cozy family business would seem to be part of the company's image and business strategy.

There is, thus, a discrepancy between the company's public motives and the actual circumstances. IKEA's social narratives can be said to depend upon outdated points of departure. The company makes use of modernist slogans and mottos that were actually formulated in circumstances that are different from those obtaining today. The rhetoric should be seen as a product of the time. One has to take into account the lack of housing and a much poorer material standard of living than we are familiar with today. During the early part of the twentieth century there were demands for a sort of democratization of beauty. Many people thought that rational mass production was the solution to the problems of housing and furnishing. There were, of course, other motives besides the social and democratic aspects. But the discussion can also be linked with a different era and context. Accordingly, there is a certain anachronism between IKEA's rhetoric and actual needs.

The company provides cheap—at least for many people in the Western world— furniture and domestic utensils. But the low prices do not necessarily indicate that the motive force lies in social consciousness, nor that the operation depends on ideological conviction. IKEA's narratives signaling social responsibility can also be seen as the commercialization of a striking rhetoric. Arresting catchphrases have been converted into slogans and have become an important part of the company profile and marketing strategy which also includes positive notions like democracy. Generally speaking, democracy posits that power is sanctioned by the people in free elections and that certain freedoms and rights are guaranteed, including freedom of speech, the right of legal redress and the right to demonstrate for political ends.

In IKEA's vocabulary democracy is a matter of low prices and increased opportunities for consumption. But are low prices necessarily always good? It is possible that extremely low prices stimulate people to overconsumption. With firms like IKEA, consumption of furniture and domestic items has made huge increases. Furniture is bought and discarded at a rapid rate. And this is hardly a question of life's necessities but, rather, of exchanging new items for old ones at brief intervals. The products have a short life and this gives rise to questions of sustainability and the environment. And the low prices may actually be an illusion. For cheap products are rapidly replaced by other cheap products and so the final result may not be as cheap as one might imagine.[40]

The democratic ambitions and the social mission as presented in IKEA's profile are thus linked with the company's Swedish roots and identity. Kamprad maintains: 'Why do we wish to emphasise our Swedish roots? Because Swedishness helps us to underline our democratic design. The democratic ideals that have developed in Sweden since the end of the 19th century are important to IKEA, because we are for the many.'[41] In his book *IKEA at Liljevalchs* (2009) Staffan Bengtsson went a few steps further, claiming that: 'Side by side with national political programmes, the company has slogged away to realise its founder's project: to be for the many people by the means of, as they say, a democratic design . . . Now when ideologies crumble and the red and blue chips are easily confused, Ingvar and his IKEA alone continue the community building . . .'[42]

Bengtsson basically claims that IKEA has taken over Sweden's role as a social pioneer and has shouldered responsibility for collective issues. The question then arises as to whether a low-price company can replace social services or whether consumption can be compared with building society. Swedishness, in all its forms, is part of the company's official self-image. But how Swedish is IKEA in point of fact? How much has the image of Sweden been glossed over and to what extent does this image depend on business rhetoric? How, exactly, do the company's profits contribute to the government-funded welfare that is so highly praised in the marketing strategies?

IKEA has long sought to associate itself with the positive aspects of Swedish life and the image of Sweden as a democratic and egalitarian welfare state. The social responsibility has also been used for navigating in a headwind or, more correctly, for meeting direct criticism of the company, whether this has been connected with child labor or a Nazi past. It is probable that, during its expansive phase, IKEA needed Sweden or, at least, gained from the country's economic growth. The construction industry was buoyant and purchasing power was growing rapidly. But how does the connection look today?

IKEA hardly needs Sweden as such, but it needs the image connected with Sweden. That is to say, the ideas about Swedish society in which social security, solidarity, equality and magnificent nature are central and valuable elements. Whether IKEA's vision of Sweden squares with reality seems to be of less importance to the company.

As we have noted, the corporate culture at IKEA is permeated by numerous values that are associated with Sweden. The company seeks to treat staff in an honorable manner, to maintain control of working conditions, including the conditions applying to people working for IKEA's suppliers, and it works to achieve equality. Its own image is that the company maintains a progressive attitude in these areas.[43] But regardless of whether the company is better or more forward-looking than many other companies, its narratives about Sweden and Swedish design are largely outdated or are ideas that are challenged: nostalgic flashbacks to a romanticized idyll. IKEA's policies pertaining to diversity and ethnicity can be regarded as updated narratives about Swedishness while others lag seriously behind and are controversial.

Symbols, images and narratives about a nation are important parts of a national identity. It is not geographical boundaries or genetic similarities that bind a people together but other sorts of ceremonies and narratives of a common history. National narratives frequently contain memories of a glorious past that once made this a mighty nation. In Sweden, the welfare state and the Swedish way are examples of such symbols. While France celebrates itself as a republic, Sweden prides itself on its welfare for all, a national and mythological narrative.[44] But the Swedish welfare state has never been a conflict-free zone and the image of Sweden as a highly successful country, a veritable stronghold of modernity, has been challenged.

The IKEA narrative can be read as modern Sweden's myth about itself. During the 1990s Sweden went from being a model country to becoming a welfare state in crisis. Looking back we can see that the more the welfare state was eroded—which happened in parallel with IKEA's expansion into a multinational corporation—the more IKEA stressed the notion of the Swedish welfare state. That the company explicitly and consciously presents itself as a Swedish rather than a global business is, to a large degree, a matter of differentiating itself through its narratives. IKEA constructs its own Swedish narrative, adapting it to its own self-image. IKEA's national identity can, in other words, be exchanged for Swedish currency.

The company and its narratives are also used by the Swedish government in order to give the national identity new life. Just like IKEA, Sweden can be regarded as a brand that seeks to establish its profile in the global arena. The government's eagerness to highlight IKEA illustrates the belief that success leads to success. IKEA uses pictures of Sweden in its marketing and Sweden uses IKEA. The company and the nation seem to enter into a symbiosis with advantages to both parties. The respective brand profiles have common denominators and the narratives confirm mutually established and stereotypical notions about the nation and Swedish design. The process is, in other words, reciprocal.

Just like IKEA's presentation of Swedishness, the company's self-image as innovative and pioneering, as illustrated in the narratives, can be questioned. Clever solutions to problems are credited to IKEA's distinctive way of being, and are often the result of a constant effort to reduce prices. That IKEA is innovative cannot be questioned, but it is not necessarily innovative in the way that the company claims. Reality is adapted and refined in the company's narratives. The creative and pioneering aspect is more a matter of building on traditions and developing concepts right from the start.

IKEA has been skilful at developing concepts commercially: everything from flat-pack furniture to staged presentations of furniture in the stores and the catalog. But the company's success is not just a matter of products and sales strategies. One strong suit is marketing and its corporate culture which, in turn, builds on narratives in which Swedishness and social responsibility are central elements; something that they have not always been. In the 1950s and 1960s no one at IKEA talked about social consciousness and the Swedish dimension hardly existed. At the time, product names held no associations to anything Swedish and the company name was spelt Ikéa, while the logotype remained yellow and white for many years.

During the 1970s and 1980s IKEA underwent a metamorphosis. Symbols of Swedishness and rhetoric about social ambitions were gradually introduced. With *The Testament of a Furniture Dealer* (1976) and the creation narrative *The Future is Filled with Opportunities* (1984) the foundation of the IKEA narratives was laid down. Parallel with economic success and international expansion, Swedishness and social responsibility have been renegotiated and reformulated. In the 1980s IKEA appeared to the world as the Robin Hood of the furniture industry which stole from the rich and gave to the poor. And during the 1990s, instead, the company increasingly referred to Swedish welfare policy with a focus on social security.

IKEA stores now exist in most parts of the world. The basic principles and directives for marketing are common to all the stores but the advertising differs from country to country. And, naturally, the way in which the brand is perceived differs in different national cultures. But despite these differences in how the brand is received and understood, the Swedish aspect and the social ambitions act as a global underpinning. But the extent to which the IKEA narratives conform to truth is, as noted a very different story.

Notes

1 Emile Zola, *The Ladies' Paradise* (Oxford: Oxford University Press, 2012) [1883], p. 3.

2 Emile Zola, *The Ladies' Paradise* (Oxford: Oxford University Press, 2012) [1883], p. 234.

3 The campaign was conducted by the Brindfors agency in 1989, involving a series of advertisements. Many of these can be found in the advertising archive at Landskrona Museum.

4 *Democratic Design* 1995, p. 11.

5 William Leach, 'Strategist of Display and the Production of Desire' in Simon J. Bronner (ed.), *Consuming Visions. Accumulation and Display of Goods in America 1880–1920* (New York: W.W. Norton, cop. 1989), p. 118.

6 Bengtsson also curated the IKEA exhibition at Liljevalchs. That the book lacked critical distance was noted in reviews. See Lotta Jonsson, 'Lasse Brunnström: 'Svensk designhistoria, Staffan Bengtsson: IKEA the book. Formgivare, produkter & annat,' *Dagens Nyheter*, December 16, 2010.

7 Fiell 2002, p. 280; Helgesson and Nyberg 2000, p. 35.

8 *From Ellen Key to IKEA. A Brief Journey Through the History of Everyday Articles in the 20th Century* (Gothenburg: Röhsska Museum of Art & Crafts, 1991).

9 Erika Josefsson/TT Spektra, 'IKEA ställs ut på Liljevalchs,' *Expressen*, May 28, 2009.

10 Gallery director Mårten Castenfors quoted in Erika Josefsson/TT Spektra 2009.

11 Some space was devoted to the question of whether IKEA had copied other people. At the same time the author noted that the IKEA concept had been plagiarized by the American firm STøR. The exhibition's serious lack of criticism was noted by several reviewers. See Peter Cornell, 'IKEA på Liljevalchs,' *Expressen*, June 16, 2009; Ulrika Stahre, 'Drömkonst för alla,' *Aftonbladet*, June 18, 2009; Ingrid Sommar, 'Reklam eller konst?,' *Sydsvenskan*, June 16, 2009.

12 Heiner Uber, *Democratic Design: IKEA—Möbel für die menscheit* (Exhibition Catalog: Neue Sammlung, Pinakothek der Moderne, IKEA Deutschland GmbH & Company KG, 2009).

13 Examples of corporate museums are The World of Coca-Cola, Atlanta and the Mercedes Museum, Stuttgart. IKEA has commissioned the US company Ralph Appenbaum Associates for producing museum displays.

14 Ingvar Kamprad, 'New Friends' in Bengtsson 2009. Unpaginated catalog.

15 IKEA used the term 'Democratic design' in 1995 in connection with the launch of the PS collection and the book *Democratic Design* (1995). Since then the term has been much used both internally and in marketing. See, for example, the book *Democratic Design 2013* (Älmhult: IKEA, 2012).

16 Paul Greenhalgh (ed.), *Modernism in Design* (London: Reaktion Books, 1990), p. 10.

17 In *Analytical Advertising* (1912) William A. Shryer claimed that 'it is . . . unprofitable for the advertiser to centre his appeal around copy that presumes the existence of a function so slightly developed in the average man.' Shryer quoted in T. J. Jackson Lears, 'From Salvation to Self-Realization. Advertising and the Therapeutic Roots of the Consumer Culture' in Richard Wightman Fox and T. J. Jackson Lears (eds), *The Culture of Consumption: Critical Essays in American History 1880–1980* (New York: Pantheon Books, 1983), p. 19.

18 Edward Bernays (with introduction by Mark Crispin Miller), *Propaganda*, Brooklyn, N.Y.: Ig Publishing, cop. 2005 [1928]. On Bernays' in relation to consumption see Jackson Lears, 'From Salvation to Self-Realization. Advertising and the Therapeutic Roots of the Consumer Culture' in Wightman Fox and Jackson Lears 1983, p. 20.

19 Rachel Bowlby has also noted the importance of psychology to marketing and consumption and she has shown how Freud's theories were implemented as a strategic resource during the early twentieth century. Rachel Bowlby, *Shopping with Freud* (London: Routledge, 1993).

20 Georges Perec, *Les Choses. Une histoire des années soixante* (Paris: Julliard, 1990) [1965].

21 For this and other works by Barbara Kruger commenting explicitly on consumption and economics, see Kate Linker, *Love for Sale. The Words and Pictures of Barbara Kruger* (New York: Abrams, 1990), pp. 65, 73–80.

22 For a critical survey of research into consumption in various disciplines see Daniel Miller (ed.), *Acknowledging Consumption. A Review of New Studies* (London: Routledge, 1995).

23 For a discussion of consumption as a liberating and creative force see Miller 1995, 28ff. On dreams of consumption as degenerative and stultifying see, for example, Rosalind Williams, *Dream Worlds. Mass Consumption in Late Nineteenth-Century France* (Berkeley: University of California Press, 1991) [1982]. For a discussion of theoretical perspectives in the study of consumption see Orsi Husz and Amanda Lagerqvist, 'Konsumtionens motsägelser. En inledning' in Peder Aléx and Johan Söderberg (eds), *Förbjudna njutningar* (Stockholm: Stockholms Universitet 2001).

24 Theodor W. Adorno and Max Horkheimer, *Dialectic of Enlightenment* (translated by John Cumming) (London: Verso, 1997) [1947].

25 Colin Campbell, 'I Shop Therefore I Know That I Am: The Metaphysical Basis of Modern Consumerism' in Karin M. Ekström and Helene Brembeck (eds), *Elusive Consumption* (Oxford: Berg, 2004), 27ff.

26 Wolfgang Fritz Haug, *Critique of Commodity Aesthetics: Appearance, Sexuality and Advertising in Capitalist Society* (Cambridge: Polity, cop. 1986) [1971].

27 Guy Debord, The Society of the Spectacle (translated by Donald Nicholson-Smith) (New York: Zone Books, 1994) [1967].

28 Zygmunt Bauman, *Consuming Life* (Cambridge: Polity, 2007).

29 Zygmunt Bauman, *Consuming Life* (Cambridge: Polity, 2007).

30 Chuck Palahniuk, *Fight Club* (London: Vintage Books, 2006) [1997]. The film *Fight Club* (1999) was directed by David Fincher. There are several analyses of Fight Club, for example, Henry A. Giroux, 'Brutalised Bodies and Emasculated Politics: Fight Club, Consumerism and Masculine Violence,' *Third Text*, 14: 53 (London: Kala Press, 2000), pp. 31–41.

31 Palahniuk 2006, p. 43.

32 Quote from the film *Fight Club* (1999). The remark does not appear in the novel.

33 Palahniuk 2006, pp. 110–11.

34 The phenomenon is discussed in Daniel Birnbaum, 'IKEA at the End of Metaphysics,' *Frieze*, Issue 31, Nov–Dec (1996). Another example is artist Jason Rhoades whose work included allusions to, or direct comments on, IKEA's ideology. For an exhibition (Wanås, Sweden1996) he constructed four copies of the little green shed that Kamprad had formerly used for selling products and he collected a mass of products from IKEA. During the exhibition he cut the sheds into two pieces and sliced up the furniture with a chainsaw. Other examples of Rhoades' work in which IKEA plays a prominent part are 'Swedish Erotica' (1994) and 'The Future is Filled with Possibilities' (1996).

35 Clay Ketter quoted in Åsa Nacking, 'Made Ready-Mades,' *Nu. The Nordic Art Review*, Vol. II, No. 2 (2000). At the Sydney Biennial Ketter showed an installation consisting entirely of 'Billy' bookshelves. Artist John Freyer has also worked with IKEA's products, particularly 'Billy' shelving and has collaborated with researchers in the project 'Opening the Flatpack: Ethnography, Art, and the Billy Bookcase.' See http://www.temporama.com.

36 Anders Jakobsen interviewed in Sara Kristoffersson, 'Anders Jakobsen till skogs,' *Konstnären*, No. 2 (2006). There are other examples of IKEA products being used as building materials, not all of them with a critical perspective. See http://www.IKEAhackers.net/

37 *IKEA Concept Description* 2000, p. 48 (IHA).

38 *IKEA Concept Description* 2000, p. 48

39 *IKEA Concept Description* 2000, pp. 47–8.

40 Ellen Ruppel Shell, *Cheap. The High Cost of Discount Culture* (New York: Penguin Press, 2009).

41 Ingvar Kamprad, 'New Friends' in Bengtsson 2009. Unpaginated.

42 Bengtsson 2009. Unpaginated catalog.

43 Interview Helene Duphorn, Lena Simonsson-Berge, June 25, 2013.

44 Andersson 2009:1; Andersson 2009:2.

REFERENCES

Archives

IKEA Historical Archives (IHA)

10 Years of Stories From IKEA People, Inter IKEA Systems B.V., 2008.
1700-tal, Inter IKEA Systems B.V., 1996.
Challenge/Solution, Postcard, Inter IKEA Systems, B.V., 2010.
Democratic design. The Story About the Three Dimensional World of IKEA—Form, Function and Low Prices, Inter IKEA Systems B.V., 1996.
Designed for People. Swedish Home Furnishing 1700–2000, Inter IKEA Systems B.V., 1999.
IKEA Catalogue, 1955.
IKEA Concept Description, Inter IKEA Systems B.V., 2000.
IKEA Match.
IKEA Stories 1 (DVD), Inter IKEA Systems B.V., 2005, 2008.
IKEA Stories 1, Inter IKEA Systems B.V., 2005.
IKEA Stories 3, Inter IKEA Systems B.V., 2006.
IKEA Tillsammans, Inter IKEA Systems B.V., 2011.
IKEA Toolbox (intranet).
IKEA Values. An Essence of the IKEA Concept, Inter IKEA Systems B.V., 2007.
IKEAs rötter. Ingvar Kamprad berättar om tiden 1926–1986 (DVD), Inter IKEA Systems B.V., 2007.
Ingvar Kamprad: Mitt största fiasko, Letter to co-workers.
Insight, IKEA IDEAS, March 2012, Issue 87, Inter IKEA Systems B.V., 2012.
Marketing Communication. The IKEA Way, Inter IKEA Systems B.V., 2010.
Our Way Forward. The Brand Values Behind the IKEA Concept, Inter IKEA Systems B.V., 2011.
Our Way. The Brand Values Behind the IKEA Concept, Inter IKEA Systems B.V., 2008 (2nd edition) [1999].
PS, Inter IKEA Systems B.V., 1996.
Scandinavian Collections 1996–97 (DVD), Inter IKEA Systems B.V., 1997.
Stockholm, Inter IKEA Systems B.V., 1996
The Future is Filled With Opportunities. The Story Behind the Evolution of the IKEA Concept, Inter IKEA Systems B.V., 2008 [1984].
The IKEA Concept, The Testament of A Furniture Dealer, A Little IKEA Dictionary, Inter IKEA Systems B.V., 2011 [1976–2011].
The Origins of the IKEA Culture and Values, Inter IKEA Systems B.V., 2012
The Stone Wall—a Symbol of the IKEA Culture, Inter IKEA Systems B.V., 2012.
Vackrare vardag, Inter IKEA Systems, B.V., Produced by Brindfors, 1990.
Oral information, Hugo Sahlin.

National Library Sweden, Stockholm (NLC)

IKEA symbolerna. Att leda med exempel, Inter IKEA Systems B.V., 2001.
Range Presentation, Inter IKEA Systems B.V., 2000, 2001.
Range Presentation, Inter IKEA Systems B.V., 2002.

Library of the Ministry for Foreign Affairs, Stockholm (LMFA)

Främjandeplan Bangkok 2011–2013, Sveriges Ambassad Bangkok, Utrikesdepartementet, Dnr.
    UF 2010/66885/FIM, Kat: 4.5.
Främjandeplan Belgrad 2011–2013, Sveriges Ambassad Belgrad, Utrikesdepartementet, Dnr. UF
    2010/68999/FIM, Kat: 4.5.
Främjandeplan Grekland 2011–2013, Sveriges Ambassad Athen, Utrikesdepartementet, Dnr. UF
    2010/68981/FIM, Kat: 4.5.
Främjandeplan för Island 2011–2013, Sveriges Ambassad Reykjavik, Utrikesdepartementet, Dnr.
    UF 2010/66980/FIM: Kat, 4.5.
Främjandeplan Jordanien 2011–2013, Sveriges Ambassad Amman, Utrikesdepartementet, Dnr.
    UF 2010/68979/FIM, Kat: 4.5.
Främjandeplan Lissabon 2011–2013, Sveriges Ambassad Lissabon, Utrikesdepartementet, Dnr.
    UF2010/71903/FIM, Kat: 4.5.
Främjandeplan Ryssland 2011–2013, Sveriges Ambassad Moskva, Utrikesdepartementet Dnr.
    UF2010/69681/FIM, Kat: 4.5.
Främjandeplan Singapore 2011–2013, Sveriges Ambassad Singapore, Utrikesdepartementet, Dnr.
    UF 2010/66401/FIM, Kat: 4.5.
Främjandeplan Tel Aviv 2011–2013, Sveriges Ambassad Tel Aviv, Utrikesdepartementet, Dnr. UF
    2010/69971/FIM, Kat: 4.5.

Reklamarkivet, Landskrona Museum, Landskrona (LM)

Advertisements 1980 and 1990s.

Hans Brindfors, Private collection

Advertisements 1980 and 1990s.

Interviews

Mats Agmén, Managing IKEA Concept Monitoring, Inter IKEA Systems B.V., interviewed by the
    author, Helsingborg, September 21, 2012.
Hans Brindfors, interviewed by the author, January 20, 2012.
Ulla Christiansson, interviewed by the author, Stockholm, December 22, 2011.
Helen Duphorn, Head of Corporate Communication, IKEA Group and Lena Simonsson-Berge,
    Global Communication Manager, IKEA Retail Services, interviewed by the author, Helsingborg,
    June 25, 2013.
Lennart Ekmark, interviewed by the author, Stockholm, December 16, 2011.

Lennart Ekmark, Lea Kumpulainen, Range Strategist, interviewed by the author, Stockholm, June 12, 2009.
Per Hahn, Senior Manager IKEA Culture and Values, interviewed by the author, Älmhult, June 26, 2012.
Ola Lindell, Senior Manager Marketing, interviewed by the author, Stockholm, November 9, 2011.
Lismari Markgren, Inter IKEA Systems B.V., interviewed by the author, Waterloo, January 4, 2011.

Film and TV

Adapation, Director Spike Jonze, 2002.
Fight Club, Director David Fincher, 1999.
Rakt på sak med K-G Bergström, Sveriges Television, 2008.
Uppdrag granskning. Made in Sweden—IKEA, Producer Nils Hansson, Sveriges Television, 2011.
Två världsföretag. Tomtens verkstad—IKEAs bakgård, Producer Andreas Franzén, Sveriges Television, 1997.

Correspondence

Ola Lindell, August 20, 2013.
Ola Lindell, November 9, 2013.

Other

Ingvar Kamprad: *Framtidens IKEA-varuhus* daterat, October 10, 1989. Document given to the author by a former IKEA-employee.
Livet hemma, Document given to the author by Lennart Ekmark.
Participation in intern course, *The IKEA Brand Programme 2012*, Inter IKEA Culture Center, Älmhult.

Internet

Dates and addresses can be found in the footnotes.
http://www.benjerry.com
http://www.coca-colacompany.com
http://www.cremedelamer.com
http://www.designaret.se
http://www.historyfactory.com
http://www.how-to-branding.com
http://www.ikea.com
http://www.ikeahackers.net
http://www.regeringen.se
http://www.simonanholt.com
http://www.sweden.se
http://www.temporama.com
http://www.visitsweden.com

Bibliography

Adorno, T. W. and Horkheimer, M., *Dialectic of Enlightenment*, London: Verso, 1997 [1947].

Ahl, Z. and Olsson, E., *Svensk smak. Myter om den moderna formen*, Stockholm: Ordfront, 2001.

Aléx, P., *Den rationella konsumenten. KF som folkuppfostrare 1899–1939*, Diss., Stockholm: B. Östlings bokförlag. Symposion, 1994.

Almqvist, K. and Linklater, A. (eds), *Images of Sweden*, Stockholm: Axel and Margaret Ax:son Johnson Foundation, 2011.

Anderby, O., 'Intervju med Lennart Ekmark. Om reklam i allmänhet—om IKEA:s i synnerhet,' 4/5, *Den svenska marknaden* (1983).

Anderson, B., *Imagined Communities. Reflections on the Origin and Spread of Nationalism*, Verso, London, 1983.

Andersson, F., *Performing Co-Production. On the Logic and Practice of Shopping at IKEA*, Diss., Uppsala: Department of Social and Economic Geography, Uppsala University, 2009.

Andersson, J., *När framtiden redan hänt. Socialdemokratin och folkhemsnostalgin*, Stockholm: Ordfront, 2009. (1)

Andersson, J., 'Nordic Nostalgia and Nordic Light. The Swedish Model as Utopia 1930–2007,' *Scandinavian Journal of History*, 34 (3) (2009). (2)

Andersson, J. and Hilson, M., 'Images of Sweden and the Nordic Countries,' *Scandinavian Journal of History*, 34, (3) (2009).

Andersson, J. and Östberg, K., *Sveriges historia 1965–2012*, Stockholm: Norstedts, 2013.

Andersson, O., 'Saker som får oss att vilja röka crack: SAS nya designprofil,' *Bibel* 5 (1999).

Andersson, O., 'Folkhemsbygget i KF:s regi,' *Svenska Dagbladet*, June 11, 2004.

Anholt, S., *Brand America. The Mother of All Brands*, London: Cyan, 2004.

Anholt, S., *Competitive Identity. The Brand Management for Nations, Cities and Regions*, New York: Palgrave Macmillan, 2007.

Arnstberg, K. O., *Miljonprogrammet*, Stockholm: Carlssons Bokförlag, 2000.

Aronczyk, M., *Branding the Nation: The Global Business of National Identity*, Oxford University Press, 2013.

Åsbrink, E., *Och i Wienerwald står träden kvar*, Stockholm: Natur & Kultur, 2012.

Asplund, G., Gahn, W., Markelius, S., Sundahl, E. and Åhrén, U., 'acceptera' [1931] in L. Creagh, H. Kåberg and B. Miller Lane (eds), *Modern Swedish Design. Three Founding Texts*, New York: Museum of Modern Art, 2008.

Atle Bjarnestam, E., *IKEA. Design och identitet*, Malmö: Arena, 2009.

Barthes, R., *Mythologies*, New York: Hill and Wang, 2012 [1957].

Bartlett C. A. and Nanda A., *Ingvar Kamprad and IKEA*, Harvard Business Publishing, Premier Case, 1990.

Bauman, Z., *Consuming Life*, Cambridge: Polity, 2007.

Beckman, U., 'Dags för design,' *Form* 2 (1995).

Bengtsson, S. (ed.), *IKEA at Liljevalchs*, Stockholm: Liljevalchs konsthall, 2009.

Bengtsson, S., *IKEA The Book. Designers, Products and Other Stuff*, Stockholm: Arvinius, 2010.

Berggren, H., 'Ideologin som gick hem,' *Dagens Nyheter*, August 30, 1998.

Bernays, E. (with introduction by Mark Crispin Miller): *Propaganda*, Brooklyn, N.Y.: Ig Publishing, cop. 2005 [1928].

BILLY—30 år med BILLY, Produced by IMP Books AB for IKEA FAMILY, 2009.

Birnbaum, D., 'IKEA at the End of Metaphysics,' *Frieze*, Issue 31, Nov–Dec (1996).

Birnbaum, D., 'Läran lyder: Billy,' *Dagens Nyheter*, August 30, 1998.

Björk, S., *IKEA. Entreprenören. Affärsidén. Kulturen*, Stockholm: Svenska Förlaget, 1998.

Björk, S., Dahlgren, L. and von Schulzenheim, C., *IKEA mot framtiden*, Stockholm: Norstedts, 2013.

Björkvall, A., 'Practical Function and Meaning. A case study of IKEA tables,' in C. Jewitt (ed.), *The Routledge Handbook of Multimodal Analysis*, London: Routledge, 2009.

Björling, S., 'IKEA—Alla tiders katalog,' *Dagens Nyheter*, August 10, 2010.

Boisen, L. A., *Reklam. Den goda kraften*, Stockholm: Ekerlids förlag, 2003.

Boje, D. M., 'Stories of the Storytelling Organization: A Postmodern Analysis of Disney as "Tamara-Land",' *Academy of Management Journal*, 38, (4) (1995).

Boman, M. (ed.), *Svenska möbler 1890–1990*, Lund: Signum, 1991.

Boman, M., 'Den kluvna marknaden' in M. Boman (ed.), *Svenska möbler 1890–1990*, Lund: Signum, 1991.

Boman, M., 'Vardagens decennium' in M. Boman (ed.), *Svenska möbler 1890–1990*, Lund: Signum, 1991.

Bowallius, M-L. and Toivio, M., 'Mäktiga märken' in Holger, L. and Ingalill Holmberg, I. (eds), *Identitet. Om varumärken, tecken och symboler*, Stockholm: Raster, 2002.

Bowlby, R., *Shopping with Freud*, London: Routledge, 1993.

Brown, A., *Fishing in Utopia*, 2008, London: Granta, 2008.

Brûlé, T., 'Blondes do it Better,' *Wallpaper*, 14 (1998).

Brunnström, L., *Det svenska folkhemsbygget. Om Kooperativa förbundets arkitektkontor*, Stockholm: Arkitektur, 2004.

Brunnström, L., *Svensk designhistoria*, Stockholm: Raster, 2010.

Cabra, R. and Nelson, K. E. (eds), *New Scandinavian Design*, San Francisco: Chronicle Books, 2004.

Campbell, C., 'I Shop Therefore I Know That I Am: The Metaphysical Basis of Modern Consumerism' in Ekström, K. M. and Brembeck, H. (eds), *Elusive Consumption*, Oxford: Berg, 2004.

Carp, O., 'Inga kvinnor i saudisk Ikeakatalog,' *Dagens Nyheter*, October 1, 2012.

Childs, M. W., *Sweden. The Middle Way*, New Haven: Yale, 1936.

Clark, H. and Brody, D. (eds), *Design Studies. A Reader*, Oxford: Berg Publishers, 2009.

Clemens, J. K. and Mayer, D. F., *The Classic Touch: Lessons in Leadership from Homer to Hemingway* (New York: McGraw-Hill, 1999).

Coley, C., 'Furniture: Design, Manufacture, Marketing' in Alexander von Vegesack (ed.), *Jean Prouvé. The Poetics of the Technical Object*, Weil am Rhein: Vitra Design Stiftung, 2006.

Cornell, P., 'IKEA på Liljevalchs,' *Expressen*, June 16, 2009.

Corrigan, P., *Shakespeare on Management. Leadership Lessons for Today's Managers*, London: Kogan Page Business Books, 1999.

Cracknell, A., *The Real Mad Men. The Remarkable True Story of Madison Avenue's Golden Age, When a Handful of Renegades Changed Advertising for Ever*, London: Quercus, 2011.

Crowley, D. and Pavitt, J. (eds), *Cold War Modern. Design 1945–1970*, London: V&A Publishing, 2008.

Czarniawska, B., *Narrating the Organization: Dramas on Institutional Identity*, Chicago: University of Chicago Press, 1997.

Dagens Industri, December 17, 1981.

Dahlgren, L., *IKEA älskar Ryssland. En berättelse om ledarskap, passion och envishet*, Stockholm: Natur & Kultur, 2009.

Dahlvig, A., *Med uppdrag att växa. Om ansvarsfullt företagande*, Lund: Studentlitteratur, 2011.

Daun, Å., *Svensk mentalitet. Ett jämförande perspektiv*, Stockholm: Rabén & Sjögren, 1989.

Debord, G., *The Society of the Spectacle*, New York: Zone Books, 1994 [1967].

Delanty, G. and Kumar, K. (eds), *The SAGE Handbook of Nations and Nationalism*, London: SAGE, 2006.

Democratic Design. A Book About Form, Function and Price—Three Dimensions at IKEA, Älmhult: IKEA, 1995.

Democratic design 2013, Älmhult: IKEA, 2012.

Demokrati och makt i Sverige, Stockholm: Allmänna förlaget, Statens offentliga utredningar, SOU, 1990:44.

Ehn, B., Frykman, J. and Löfgren, O., *Försvenskningen av Sverige. Det nationellas förvandlingar*, Stockholm: Natur & Kultur, 1993.

Eriksson, E., *Den moderna staden tar form. Arkitektur och debatt 1919–1935*, Stockholm: Ordfront, 2001.

Fallan, K., *Design History. Understanding Theory and Method*, Oxford: Berg Publishers, 2010.

Fallan, K. (ed.), *Scandinavian Design. Alternative Histories*, Oxford: Berg, 2012.

Fan, Y., 'Branding the nation: What is being branded?' *Journal of Vacation Marketing*, 12 (1) (2006).

Fan, Y., 'Branding the nation. Towards a Better Understanding,' *Place Branding and Public Diplomacy*, 6 (2010).

Fiell, C. and Fiell, P., *Scandinavian Design*, Köln: Taschen, 2002.

Fog K., Budtz, C., Munch, P. and Yakaboylus, B., *Storytelling. Branding in Practice*, Berlin: Springer, 2010 [2003].

Franke, B., 'Tyskarna har hittat sin Bullerbü,' *Svenska Dagbladet*, December 9, 2007.

From Ellen Key to IKEA. A Brief Journey Through the History of Everyday Articles in the 20th Century, Göteborg: Röhsska Museum of Art & Crafts, 1991.

Fryer, B., 'Storytelling That Moves People,' *Harvard Business Review*, June (2003).

Frykman, J., 'Swedish Mentality. Between Modernity and Cultural Nationalism' in Almqvist, K. and Glans, K. (eds), *The Swedish Success Story*, Stockholm: Axel and Margaret Ax:son Johnson Foundation, 2004.

Gabriel, Y., *Storytelling in Organizations: Facts, Fictions, and Fantasies*, Oxford: Oxford University Press, 2000.

Galli, R., *Varumärkenas fält. Produktion av erkännande i Stockholms reklamvärld*, Diss., Stockholm: Acta Universitatis Stockholmiensis, 2012.

Garvey, P., 'Consuming IKEA. Inspiration as Material Form,' in Clarke, A. J. (ed.), *Design Anthropology*, Wien, New York: Springer Verlag, 2010.

Ghoshal, S. and Bartlett, C. A., *The Individualized Corporation. A Fundamentally New Approach to Management. Great Companies Defined by Purpose, Process, and People*, New York: Harper Business, 1997.

Giddens, A., *Modernity and Self-Identity: Self and Society in the Late Modern Age*, Cambridge: Polity Press, 1991.

Giroux, H. A., 'Brutalised Bodies and Emasculated Politics: Fight Club, Consumerism and Masculine Violence,' *Third Text*, 14: 53, London: Kala Press (2000).

Glaser, M., *Art is Work. Graphic Design, Objects and Illustration*, London: Thames & Hudson, 2000.

Glover, N., *National Relations. Public Diplomacy, National Identity and the Swedish Institute 1945–1970*, Diss., Lund: Nordic Academic Press, 2011.

Göransdotter, M., 'Smakfostran och heminredning. Om estetiska diskurser och bildning till bättre boende i Sverige 1930–1955' in Söderberg, J. and Magnusson, L. (eds), *Kultur och konsumtion i Norden 1750–1950*, Helsingfors: FHS, 1997.

Greenhalgh, P. (ed.), *Modernism in Design*, London: Reaktion Books, 1990.

Gremler, Dwayne D., Gwinner, K. P. and Brown, S. W. (2001), 'Generating Positive Word-of-Mouth Communication Through Customer–Employee Relationships,' *International Journal of Service Industry Management*, 12 (1) (2001).

Hagströmer, D., *Swedish Design*, Stockholm: Swedish Institute, 2001.

Hagströmer, D., 'An Experiment's Indian Summer. The Formes Scandinaves Exhibition' in W. Halén and K. Wickman (eds), Scandinavian Design Beyond the Myth. Fifty years of Design From the Nordic Countries, Stockholm: Arvinius, 2003.

Halén, W. and Wickman K. (eds), *Scandinavian Design Beyond the Myth. Fifty years of Design From the Nordic Countries*, Stockholm: Arvinius, 2003.

Hall, P., *The Social Construction of Nationalism. Sweden as an Example*, Diss., Lund: University Press, 1998.

Hamilton, C., *Historien om flaskan*, Stockholm: Norstedts, 1994.

Hård af Segerstad, U., *Scandinavian Design*, Stockholm: Nord, 1962.

Hartman, T., 'On the IKEAization of France,' *Public Culture*, 19 (3), Duke University Press (2007).

Hartwig, W. and Schug, A., *History Sells!: Angewandte Geschichte ALS Wissenschaft Und Markt*, Stuttgart: Franz Steiner Verlag, 2009.

Harvard Business Review on Corporate Responsibility, Boston: Harvard Business School, 2003.

Harvey, D., 'From Managerialism to Entrepreneurialism: The Transformation in Urban Governance in Late Capitalism,' *Geografiska Annaler. Series B, Human Geography*, 71 (1) (1989).

Haug, W. F., *Critique of Commodity Aesthetics: Appearance, Sexuality and Advertising in Capitalist Society*, Cambridge: Polity, cop. 1986 [1971].

Heath, J. and Potter, A., *The Rebel Sell: How the Counterculture Became Consumer Culture*, Chichester: Capstone, 2005.

Hedqvist, H., *1900–2002. Svensk form. Internationell design*, Stockholm: Bokförlaget DN, 2002.

Heijbel, M., *Storytelling befolkar varumärket*, Stockholm: Blue Publishing, 2010.

Helgesson, S. and Nyberg, K., *Svenska former*, Stockholm: Prisma, 2000.

Heller, S., *Paul Rand*, London: Phaidon, 2007.

Heller, S., *Iron fists. Branding the 20th-Century Totalitarian State*, London: Phaidon, 2008.

Hemmungs Wirtén, E. and Skarrie Wirtén, S., *Föregångarna. Design management i åtta svenska företag*, Stockholm: Informationsförlaget, 1989.

Hirdman, Y., *Att lägga livet tillrätta. Studier i svensk folkhemspolitik*, Stockholm: Carlsson, 1989.

Hirdman, Y., *Vi bygger landet. Den svenska arbetarrörelsens historia från Per Götrek till Olof Palme*, Stockholm: Tidens förlag, 1990 [1979].

Hirdman, Y., Björkman, J. and Lundberg U. (eds), *Sveriges Historia 1920–1965*, Stockholm: Nordstedts, 2012.

Hogdal, L., 'Demokratisk design och andra möbler,' *Arkitektur*, 4 (1995).

Howe, S., 'Untangling the Scandinavian Blonde. Modernity and the IKEA PS Range Catalogue 1995,' *Scandinavian Journal of Design*, 9 (1999).

Howkins, A., 'The Discovery of Rural England' in Colls, R. and Dodd, P. (eds), *Englishness, Politics and Culture 1880–1920*, London: Croom Helm, 1986.

Husz, O., *Drömmars värde. Varuhus och lotteri i svensk konsumtionskultur 1897–1939*, Diss., Hedemora: Gidlund, 2004.

Husz, O. and Lagerqvist, A., 'Konsumtionens motsägelser. En inledning' in Aléx, P. and Söderberg, J. (eds), *Förbjudna njutningar*, Stockholm: Stockholms Universitet, 2001.

Hyland, A. and Bateman, S., *Symbol*, London: Laurence King Publishing, 2011.

'Ikea lovade för mycket om dunet,' *Aftonbladet*, February 8, 2009.

Ivanov, G., *Vackrare vardagsvara — design för alla?: Gregor Paulsson och Svenska slöjdföreningen 1915–1925*, Diss., Umeå: Institutionen för Historiska Studier, 2004.

Jackson Lears, T. J., 'From Salvation to Self-Realization. Advertising and the Therapeutic Roots of the Consumer Culture' in Wightman Fox, R. and Jackson Lears, T. J. (eds), *The Culture of Consumption: Critical Essays in American History 1880–1980*, New York: Pantheon Books, 1983.

Jensen, R., *The Dream society. How the Coming Shift from Information to Imagination will Transform your Business*, New York: McGraw-Hill, 1999.

Johansson, G., 'Den verkliga standardmöbeln,' *Svenska Dagbladet*, July 14, 1944.

Johansson, G. (ed.), *Bostadsvanor och bostadsnormer* [Bostadsvanor i Stockholm under 1940-talet], Svenska Arkitekters Riksförbund och Svenska Slöjdföreningens Bostadsutredning, Stockholm: Kooperativa Förbundets förlag, 1964 [1955].

Jones, G., *Beauty Imagined. A History of the Global Beauty Industry*, Oxford: Oxford University Press, 2010.

Jonsson, A., *Knowledge Sharing Across Borders — A Study in the IKEA World*, Diss., Lund: Lund University School of Economics and Management, Lund Business Press, 2007.

Jonsson, L., 'Lasse Brunnström. Svensk designhistoria. Staffan Bengtsson: Ikea the book. Formgivare, produkter & annat,' *Dagens Nyheter*, December 16, 2010.

Jönsson, L. (ed.), *Craft in Dialogue. Six Views On a Practice in Change*, Stockholm: IASPIS, 2005.

Josefsson, E./TT Spektra, 'Ikea ställs ut på Liljevalchs,' *Expressen*, May 28, 2009.

Julier, G., *The Culture of Design*, London: SAGE Publications, 2000.

Kåberg, H., 'Swedish Modern. Selling Modern Sweden,' *Art Bulletin of Nationalmuseum*, 18 (2011).

Kalha, H., 'The Other Modernism: Finnish Design and National Identity' in Aav, M. and Stritzler-Levine, N. (eds), *Finnish Modern Design. Utopian Ideals and Everyday Realities, 1930–1997*, New Haven: Yale University Press, 1998.

Kalha, H., 'Just One of Those Things' — The Design in Scandinavia Exhibition 1954–57' in W. Halén and K. Wickman (eds), *Scandinavian Design Beyond the Myth. Fifty years of Design From the Nordic Countries*, Stockholm: Arvinius, 2003.

Kamprad, K., 'New Friends' in S. Bengtsson (ed.), *IKEA at Liljevalchs*, Stockholm: Liljevalchs konsthall, 2009.

Kåring Wagman, A., *Stadens melodi. Information och reklam i Stockholms kommun 1930–1980*, Diss., Stockholms universitet, Stockholm: Stockholmia, 2006.

Karlsson, J. C. H., 'Finns svenskheten? En granskning av teorier om svenskt folklynne, svensk folkkaraktär och svensk mentalitet,' *Sociologisk Forskningm*, 1 (1994).

Karlsson, K-G., *Historia som vapen: Historiebruk och Sovjetunionens upplösning 1985–1999*, Stockholm: Natur & Kultur, 1999.

Karlsson, K-G. and Zander, U. (eds), *Historien är nu: En introduktion till historiedidaktiken*, Lund: Studentlitteratur, 2004.

Kawamura, Y., *Fashion-ology. An Introduction to Fashion Studies*, Oxford: Berg, 2005.

Key, E., *The Education of the Child* (reprinted from the authorized English translation of *The Century of the Child*); with introductory note by Edward Bok, New York: G. P. Putnam's Sons, 1912 [1909, 1900].

Key, E., 'Beauty in the Home' [1899] in L. Creagh, H. Kåberg and B. Miller Lane (eds), *Modern Swedish Design. Three Founding Texts*, New York: Museum of Modern Art, 2008.

Kicherer, S., *Olivetti. A Study of the Management of Corporate Design*, London: Trefoil, 1989.

Kihlström, S., 'Ikea, Rörstrand och IT-företag har ställt ut,' *Dagens Nyheter*, January 24, 2007.

Kristoffersson, S., *Memphis och den italienska antidesignrörelsen*, Diss., Göteborg: Acta Universitatis Gothoburgensis, 2003.

Kristoffersson, S., 'Anders Jakobsen till skogs,' *Konstnären*, No. 2 (2006).

Kristoffersson, S., 'Reklamavbrott i må gott-fabriken,' *Svenska Dagbladet*, June 10, 2009.

Kristoffersson, S., 'Under strecket. Designlandet Sverige fattigt på forskning,' *Svenska Dagbladet*, November 3, 2010.

Kristoffersson, S., 'Swedish Design History,' *Journal of Design History*, 24 (2), (2011).

Kristoffersson, S. and Zetterlund, C., 'A Historiography of Scandinavian Design' in Kjetil Fallan (ed.), *Scandinavian Design. Alternative Histories*, Oxford: Berg, 2012.

Kristoffersson, S., 'Svensk form och IKEA' in J. Andersson and K. Östberg, *Sveriges historia 1965–2012*, Stockholm: Norstedts, 2013.

Larsson, L., *Varje människa är ett skåp*, Stockholm: Trevi, 1991.

Larsson, O., Johansson, L. and Larsson, L-O, *Smålands historia*, Lund: Historia Media, 2006.

Leach, W., 'Strategist of Display and the Production of Desire' in Bronner, S. J. (ed.), *Consuming Visions. Accumulation and Display of Goods in America 1880–1920*, New York: W.W. Norton, cop. 1989.

Lees-Maffei, G. and Houze, R. (eds), *The Design History Reader*, Oxford: Berg Publishers, 2010.

Lewenhagen, J., 'Ikea bekräftar: Politiska fångar användes i produktionen,' *Dagens Nyheter*, November 16, 2012.

Lewis, E., *Great IKEA! A Brand for All the People*, London: Marshall Cavendish, 2008.

Lewis, R. W., *Absolut Book. The Absolut Vodka Advertising Story*, Boston, Mass: Journey Editions, 1996.

Lind, I., 'Kamprad formar en ny världsmedelklass,' *Dagens Nyheter*, August 30, 1998.

Lindberg, H., *Vastakohtien IKEA. IKEAn arvot ja mentaliteetti muuttuvassa ajassa ja ympäristössä*, Diss., Jyväskylä; 2006: Jyväskylän yliopisto, 2006.

Lindeborg, Å., *Socialdemokraterna skriver historia. Historieskrivning som ideologisk maktresurs 1892–2000*, Diss., Stockholm: Atlas, 2001.

Linker, K., *Love for Sale. The Words and Pictures of Barbara Kruger*, New York: Abrams, 1990.

Löfgren, M., 'IKEA über alles,' *Dagens Nyheter*, August 30, 1998.

Londos, E., *Uppåt väggarna. En etnologisk studie av bildbruk*, Diss., Stockholm: Carlsson/Jönköping läns museum, 1993.

Lowry Miller, K., Piore, A. and Theil, S., 'The Teflon Shield, *Newsweek*, March 12, 137 (11) (2001).

Lundberg, U. and Tydén, M. (eds), *Sverigebilder. Det nationellas betydelser i politik och vardag*, Stockholm: Institutet för Framtidsstudier, 2008.

Lundberg, U. and Tydén, M., 'Stat och individ i svensk välfärdspolitisk historieskrivning,' *Arbejderhistoria*, 2 (2008).

Lundberg, U. and Tydén, M., 'In Search of the Swedish Model. Contested Historiography' in Mattsson, H. and Wallenstein, S-O. (eds), *Swedish Modernism. Architecture, Consumption and the Welfare State*, London: Black Dog, 2010.

Malik, N., 'No women please, we're Saudi Arabian Ikea,' *Guardian*, October 2, 2012.

Mattsson, H. and Wallenstein, S-O., *1930/1931. Den svenska modernismen vid vägskälet = Swedish Modernism at the Crossroads = Der Schwedische Modernismus am Scheideweg*, Stockholm: Axl Books, 2009.

Mattsson, H., 'Designing the "Consumer in Infinity": The Swedish Cooperative Union's New Consumer Policy, c.1970,' in Kjetil Fallan (ed.), *Scandinavian Design. Alternative Histories*, Oxford: Berg, 2012.

Mazur, J., *Die 'schwedische' Lösung: Eine kultursemiotisch orientierte Untersuchung der audiovisuellen Werbespots von IKEA in Deutschland*, Diss., Uppsala: Department of Modern Languages, Uppsala University, 2012.

McGuire, S., 'Shining Stockholm,' *Newsweek*, February 7, 2000.

McLellan, H., 'Corporate Storytelling Perspectives,' *Journal for Quality & Participation* 29 (1), (2006).

Metzger, J., *I köttbullslandet: konstruktionen av svenskt och utländskt på det kulinariska fältet*, Diss., Stockholm: Acta Universitatis Stockholmiensis, 2005.

Miller, D. (ed.), *Acknowledging Consumption. A Review of New Studies*, London: Routledge, 1995.

Moilanen, T. and Rainisto, S., *How to Brand Nations, Cities and Destinations. A Planning Book for Place Branding*, Basingstoke: Palgrave Macmillan, 2009.

Mollerup, P., *Marks of Excellence. The Function and Variety of Trademarks*, London: Phaidon, 1997.

Mossberg, L. and Nissen Johansen, E., *Storytelling*, Lund: Studentlitteratur, 2006.

Nacking, Å., 'Made Ready-Mades,' *Nu. The Nordic Art Review* 2 (2) (2000).

Nelson, K. E., *New Scandinavian Design*, San Francisco: Chronicle Books, 2004.

Nietzsche, F., *The Use and Abuse of History*, New York: Cosimo, 2005 [1874].

Nordlund, C., 'Att lära känna sitt land och sig själv. Aspekter på konstitueringen av det svenska nationallandskapet' in Eliasson, P. and Lisberg Jensen, E. (eds), *Naturens nytta*, Lund: Historiska Media, 2000.

Normann, R. and Ramirez, R., 'Designing Interactive strategy. From Value Chain to Value Constellation,' *Harvard Business Review*, July (1993).

Nye, J., *Soft Power. The Means to Success in World Politics*, New York: Perseus Books, 2004.

O'Dell, T., 'Junctures of Swedishness. Reconsidering representations of the National,' *Ethnologia Scandinavica*, Lund: Folklivsarkivet, 1998.

Olins, W., *Trading Identities: Why Countries and Companies are Taking on Each Others' Roles*, London: Foreign Policy Centre, 1999.

Översyn av myndighetsstrukturen för Sverige-, handels- och investeringsfrämjande, Departementserie 2011: 29, Utrikesdepartementet, Government Offices of Sweden.

Palahniuk, C., *Fight Club*, London: Vintage Books, 2006 [1997].

Papanek, V., 'IKEA and the Future: A Personal View' in *Democratic Design*, 1995.

Perec, G., *Les Choses. Une histoire des années soixante*, Paris: Julliard, 1990 [1965].

Persson, F., 'Ikeas platta försvar av straffarbete,' *Aftonbladet*, November 12, 2012.

Petersson, M., *Identitetsföreställningar. Performance, normativitet och makt ombord på SAS och AirHoliday*, Diss., Göteborgs universitet, Göteborg: Mara, 2003.

Pettersson, T., 'Så spred IKEA den svenska köttbullen över världen,' *Expressen*, February 21, 2011.

Polite, O., 'Global hissmusik på var mans vägg,' *Dagens Nyheter*, October 23, 2004.

Polster, B. (ed.), *Designdirectory Scandinavia*, London: Pavilion, 1999.

Porter, M. E., 'What is Strategy?', *Harvard Business Review*, Boston: Harvard Business School, Nov–Dec (1996).

Rampell, L., *Designdarwinismen™*, Stockholm: Gábor Palotai Publisher, 2007.

Robach, C. (ed.), *Konceptdesign*, Stockholm: Nationalmuseum, 2005.

Robach, C., *Formens frigörelse. Konsthantverk och design under debatt i 1960-talets Sverige*, Diss., Stockholm: Arvinius, 2010.

Rudberg, E., *Stockholmsutställningen 1930. Modernismens genombrott i svensk arkitektur*, Stockholm: Stockholmania, 1999.

Ruppel Shell, E., *Cheap. The High Cost of Discount Culture*, New York: Penguin Press, 2009.

Salmon, C., *Storytelling. Bewitching the Modern Mind*, London: Verso Books, 2010 [2007].

Salzer, M., *Identity Across Borders: A Study in the 'IKEA-World,'* Diss., Linköping: Univ., 1994.

Salzer-Mörling, M., *Företag som kulturella uttryck*, Bjärred: Academia adacta, 1998.

Salzer-Mörling, M., 'Storytelling och varumärken' in Christensen L. and Kempinsky P. (eds), *Att mobilisera för regional tillväxt*, Lund: Studentlitteratur, 2004.

Sandomirskaja, I., 'IKEA's pererstrojka,' *Moderna Tider*, November (2000).

Schroeder, J. E. and Salzer-Mörling, M. (eds), *Brand Culture*, London: Routledge, 2006.

Selkurt, C., 'Design for a Democracy' in W. Halén and K. Wickman (eds), *Scandinavian Design Beyond the Myth. Fifty years of Design From the Nordic Countries*, Stockholm: Arvinius, 2003.

Sjöberg, T., *Ingvar Kamprad och hans IKEA. En svensk saga*, Stockholm: Gedin, 1998.

Sjöholm, G., 'Fördjupar bilden av Kamprads engagemang,' *Svenska Dagbladet*, August 24, 2011.

Snidare, U., 'Han möblerar världens rum,' 23/33, *VI*, (1993).

Sommar, I., 'Reklam eller konst?,' *Sydsvenskan*, June 16, 2009.

Sparke, P., *An Introduction to Design and Culture. 1900 to the Present*, London: Routledge, 2004.

Stahre, U., 'Drömkonst för alla,' *Aftonbladet*, June 18, 2009.

Stavenow-Hidemark, E., 'IKEA satsar på svenskt 1700-tal,' *Hemslöjden* 5 (1993).

Stenebo, J., *Sanningen om IKEA*, Västerås: ICA Bokförlag, 2009.

Strannegård, L., 'Med uppdrag att berätta' in Dahlvig A., *Med uppdrag att växa. Om ansvarsfullt företagande*, Lund: Studentlitteratur, 2011.

Sundbärg, G., *Det svenska folklynnet*, Stockholm: Norstedts, 1911.

Svenska Dagbladet, 'Kamprad medger stiftelse utomlands,' January 26, 2011.

Svenska folkets möbelminnen, Ödåkra: IKEA, Inter IKEA Systems B.V., 2008.

Svenskt 1700-tal på IKEA i samarbete med Riksantikvarieämbetet, Älmhult: Inter IKEA Systems/ Riksantikvarieämbetet, 1993.

Svensson, P., 'Striden om historien. Historieätarna,' *Magasinet Arena*, 1 (2013).

Swanberg, L. K., 'Ingvar Kamprad. Patriarken som älskar att kramas' *Family Magazine*, 2 (1998).

Thiberg, S., 'Dags att undvara. 1970-talet: Insikt om de ändliga resurserna' in K. Wickman, *IKEA PS. Forum för design*, Älmhult, IKEA of Sweden, 1995.

Torekull, B., *Historien om IKEA*, Stockholm: Wahlström & Widstrand, 2008 [1998].

Torekull, B. (foreword), *Kamprads lilla gulblå. De bästa citaten från ett 85-årigt entreprenörskap*, Stockholm: Ekerlid, 2011.

Turistfrämjande för ökad tillväxt, Statens offentliga utredningar, SOU 2004:17, Näringsdepartementet, Government Offices of Sweden.

Uber, H., *Democratic Design: IKEA—Möbel für die menscheit, 2009*, Exhibition Catalogue: Neue Sammlung, Pinakothek der Moderne, IKEA Deutschland GmbH & Company KG, 2009.

van Belleghen, S., *The Conversation Company. Boost Your Business Through Culture, People & Social Media*, London: Kogan Page, 2012.

van Ham, P., 'The Rise of the Brand State,' Council of Foreign Relations, *Foreign Affairs*, September/October (2001).

Vinterhed, K., *Gustav Jonsson på Skå. En epok i svensk barnavård*, Diss., Stockholm: Tiden, 1977.

Wallpaper, 'Design guide Stockholm,' No. 11 (1998).

Wästberg, O., 'The Symbiosis of Sweden & IKEA,' *Public Diplomacy Magazine*, University of Southern California, Issue 2 (2009).

Wästberg, O., 'The Lagging Brand of Sweden' in Almqvist, K. and Linklater, A. (eds), *Images of Sweden*, Stockholm: Axel and Margaret Ax:son Johnson Foundation, 2011.

Werner, J., *Medelvägens estetik. Sverigebilder i USA Del 1*, Hedemora/Möklinta: Gidlunds, 2008. (1)

Werner, J., *Medelvägens estetik. Sverigebilder i USA Del 2*, Hedemora/Möklinta: Gidlunds, 2008. (2)

Werther, C., 'Cool Britannia, the Millennium Dome and the 2012 Olympics, *Moderna Språk* 11 (2011).

Wickman, K., *IKEA PS. Forum för design*, Älmhult, IKEA of Sweden, 1995.

Wickman, K., 'A Furniture Store for Everyone' in S. Bengtsson (ed.), *IKEA at Liljevalchs*, Stockholm: Liljevalchs konsthall, 2009.

Wigerfeldt, A., *Mångfald och svenskhet: en paradox inom IKEA*. Malmö Institute for Studies of Migration, Diversity and Welfare (MIM), Malmö University, 2012.

Williams, R., *Dream Worlds. Mass Consumption in Late Nineteenth-Century France*, Berkeley: University of California Press, 1991 [1982].

Wilson, E., *Adorned in Dreams. Fashion and Modernity*, London: Virago, 1985.

Zetterlund, C., *Design i informationsåldern. Om strategisk design, historia och praktik*, Diss., [2003]. Stockholm: Raster, 2002.

Zetterström, J., 'Hjärnorna bakom SAS nya ansikte,' *Dagens industri*, May 21, 2001.

Zola, E., *The Ladies' Paradise*, Oxford: Oxford University Press, 2012.

INDEX